FreeBSD Documentation Project Primer for New Contributors

FreeBSD Documentation Project Primer for New Contributors

Revision: 51370
2018-01-06 23:20:15 by eadler.
Copyright © 1998, 1999, 2000, 2001, 2002, 2003, 2004, 2005, 2006, 2007, 2008, 2009, 2010, 2011, 2012, 2013, 2014, 2015, 2016, 2017 DocEng

Abstract

Thank you for becoming a part of the FreeBSD Documentation Project. Your contribution is extremely valuable, and we appreciate it.

This primer covers details needed to start contributing to the FreeBSD Documentation Project, or FDP, including tools, software, and the philosophy behind the Documentation Project.

This is a work in progress. Corrections and additions are always welcome.

Table of Contents

List of Tables

List of Examples

Preface

1. Shell Prompts

This table shows the default system prompt and superuser prompt. The examples use these prompts to indicate which type of user is running the example.

User	Prompt
Normal user	%
root	#

2. Typographic Conventions

This table describes the typographic conventions used in this book.

Meaning	Examples
The names of commands.	Use `ls -l` to list all files.
The names of files.	Edit `.login`.
On-screen computer output.	`You have mail.`
What the user types, contrasted with on-screen computer output.	`% date +"The time is %H:%M"` `The time is 09:18`
Manual page references.	Use su(1) to change user identity.
User and group names.	Only `root` can do this.
Emphasis.	The user *must* do this.
Text that the user is expected to replace with the actual text.	To search for a keyword in the manual pages, type `man -k keyword`
Environment variables.	`$HOME` is set to the user's home directory.

3. Notes, Tips, Important Information, Warnings, and Examples

Notes, warnings, and examples appear within the text.

Note

Notes are represented like this, and contain information to take note of, as it may affect what the user does.

Tip

Tips are represented like this, and contain information helpful to the user, like showing an easier way to do something.

Important

Important information is represented like this. Typically, these show extra steps the user may need to take.

Warning

Warnings are represented like this, and contain information warning about possible damage if the instructions are not followed. This damage may be physical, to the hardware or the user, or it may be non-physical, such as the inadvertent deletion of important files.

Example 1. A Sample Example

Examples are represented like this, and typically contain examples showing a walkthrough, or the results of a particular action.

4. Acknowledgments

My thanks to Sue Blake, Patrick Durusau, Jon Hamilton, Peter Flynn, and Christopher Maden, who took the time to read early drafts of this document and offer many valuable comments and criticisms.

Chapter 1. Overview

Welcome to the FreeBSD Documentation Project (FDP). Quality documentation is crucial to the success of FreeBSD, and we value your contributions very highly.

This document describes how the FDP is organized, how to write and submit documentation, and how to effectively use the available tools.

Everyone is welcome to contribute to the FDP. Willingness to contribute is the only membership requirement.

This primer shows how to:

• Identify which parts of FreeBSD are maintained by the FDP.

• Install the required documentation tools and files.

• Make changes to the documentation.

• Submit changes back for review and inclusion in the FreeBSD documentation.

1.1. Quick Start

Some preparatory steps must be taken before editing the FreeBSD documentation. First, subscribe to the FreeBSD documentation project mailing list. Some team members also interact on the #bsddocs IRC channel on EFnet. These people can help with questions or problems involving the documentation.

1. Install the textproc/docproj meta-package and Subversion. This meta-package installs all of the software needed to edit and build FreeBSD documentation. The Subversion package is needed to obtain a working copy of the documentation and generate patches with.

   ```
   # pkg install docproj subversion
   ```

2. Install a local working copy of the documentation from the FreeBSD repository in ~/doc (see Chapter 3, *The Working Copy*).

   ```
   % svn checkout https://svn.FreeBSD.org/doc/head   ~/doc
   ```

3. Configure the text editor:

   • Word wrap set to 70 characters.

   • Tab stops set to 2.

   • Replace each group of 8 leading spaces with a single tab.

   Specific editor configurations are listed in Chapter 15, *Editor Configuration*.

4. Update the local working copy:

   ```
   % svn up ~/doc
   ```

5. Edit the documentation files that require changes. If a file needs major changes, consult the mailing list for input.

   References to tag and entity usage can be found in Chapter 8, *XHTML Markup* and Chapter 9, *DocBook Markup*.

6. After editing, check for problems by running:

   ```
   % igor -R filename.xml | less -RS
   ```

Review the output and edit the file to fix any problems shown, then rerun the command to find any remaining problems. Repeat until all of the errors are resolved.

7. *Always* build-test changes before submitting them. Running **make** in the top-level directory of the documentation being edited will generate that documentation in split HTML format. For example, to build the English version of the Handbook in HTML, run `make` in the `en_US.ISO8859-1/books/handbook/` directory.

8. When changes are complete and tested, generate a "diff file":

```
% cd ~/doc
% svn diff > bsdinstall .diff.txt
```

Give the diff file a descriptive name. In the example above, changes have been made to the `bsdinstall` portion of the Handbook.

9. Submit the diff file using the web-based Problem Report system. If using the web form, enter a Summary of *[patch] short description of problem*. Select the Component `Documentation`. In the Description field, enter a short description of the changes and any important details about them. Use the [Add an attachment] button to attach the diff file. Finally, use the [Submit Bug] button to submit your diff to the problem report system.

1.2. The FreeBSD Documentation Set

The FDP is responsible for four categories of FreeBSD documentation.

* *Handbook*: The Handbook is the comprehensive online resource and reference for FreeBSD users.

* *FAQ*: The FAQ uses a short question and answer format to address questions that are frequently asked on the various mailing lists and forums devoted to FreeBSD. This format does not permit long and comprehensive answers.

* *Manual pages*: The English language system manual pages are usually not written by the FDP, as they are part of the base system. However, the FDP can reword parts of existing manual pages to make them clearer or to correct inaccuracies.

* *Web site*: This is the main FreeBSD presence on the web, visible at https://www.FreeBSD.org/ and many mirrors around the world. The web site is typically a new user's first exposure to FreeBSD.

Translation teams are responsible for translating the Handbook and web site into different languages. Manual pages are not translated at present.

Documentation source for the FreeBSD web site, Handbook, and FAQ is available in the documentation repository at `https://svn.FreeBSD.org/doc/` .

Source for manual pages is available in a separate source repository located at `https://svn.FreeBSD.org/base/` .

Documentation commit messages are visible with `svn log`. Commit messages are also archived at `http://lists.FreeBSD.org/mailman/listinfo/svn-doc-all` .

Web frontends to both of these repositories are available at https://svnweb.FreeBSD.org/doc/ and https://svnweb.FreeBSD.org/base/.

Many people have written tutorials or how-to articles about FreeBSD. Some are stored as part of the FDP files. In other cases, the author has decided to keep the documentation separate. The FDP endeavors to provide links to as much of this external documentation as possible.

Chapter 2. Tools

Several software tools are used to manage the FreeBSD documentation and render it to different output formats. Some of these tools are required and must be installed before working through the examples in the following chapters. Some are optional, adding capabilities or making the job of creating documentation less demanding.

2.1. Required Tools

Install textproc/docproj from the Ports Collection. This *meta-port* installs all the applications required to do useful work with the FreeBSD documentation. Some further notes on particular components are given below.

2.1.1. DTDs and Entities

FreeBSD documentation uses several Document Type Definitions (DTDs) and sets of XML entities. These are all installed by the textproc/docproj port.

XHTML DTD (textproc/xhtml)
 XHTML is the markup language of choice for the World Wide Web, and is used throughout the FreeBSD web site.

DocBook DTD (textproc/docbook-xml)
 DocBook is designed for marking up technical documentation. Most of the FreeBSD documentation is written in DocBook.

ISO 8879 entities (textproc/iso8879)
 Character entities from the ISO 8879:1986 standard used by many DTDs. Includes named mathematical symbols, additional characters in the Latin character set (accents, diacriticals, and so on), and Greek symbols.

2.2. Optional Tools

These applications are not required, but can make working on the documentation easier or add capabilities.

2.2.1. Software

Vim (editors/vim)
 A popular editor for working with XML and derived documents, like DocBook XML.

Emacs or XEmacs (editors/emacs or editors/xemacs)
 Both of these editors include a special mode for editing documents marked up according to an XML DTD. This mode includes commands to reduce the amount of typing needed, and help reduce the possibility of errors.

Chapter 3. The Working Copy

The *working copy* is a copy of the FreeBSD repository documentation tree downloaded onto the local computer. Changes are made to the local working copy, tested, and then submitted as patches to be committed to the main repository.

A full copy of the documentation tree can occupy 700 megabytes of disk space. Allow for a full gigabyte of space to have room for temporary files and test versions of various output formats.

Subversion is used to manage the FreeBSD documentation files. It is obtained by installing the Subversion package:

```
# pkg install subversion
```

3.1. Documentation and Manual Pages

FreeBSD documentation is not just books and articles. Manual pages for all the commands and configuration files are also part of the documentation, and part of the FDP's territory. Two repositories are involved: doc for the books and articles, and base for the operating system and manual pages. To edit manual pages, the base repository must be checked out separately.

Repositories may contain multiple versions of documentation and source code. New modifications are almost always made only to the latest version, called head.

3.2. Choosing a Directory

FreeBSD documentation is traditionally stored in /usr/doc/ , and system source code with manual pages in /usr/src/. These directory trees are relocatable, and users may want to put the working copies in other locations to avoid interfering with existing information in the main directories. The examples that follow use ~/doc and ~/src, both subdirectories of the user's home directory.

3.3. Checking Out a Copy

A download of a working copy from the repository is called a *checkout*, and done with svn checkout. This example checks out a copy of the latest version (head) of the main documentation tree:

```
% svn checkout https://svn.FreeBSD.org/doc/head    ~/doc
```

A checkout of the source code to work on manual pages is very similar:

```
% svn checkout https://svn.FreeBSD.org/base/head    ~/src
```

3.4. Updating a Working Copy

The documents and files in the FreeBSD repository change daily. People modify files and commit changes frequently. Even a short time after an initial checkout, there will already be differences between the local working copy and the main FreeBSD repository. To update the local version with the changes that have been made to the main repository, use svn update on the directory containing the local working copy:

```
% svn update ~/doc
```

Get in the protective habit of using svn update before editing document files. Someone else may have edited that file very recently, and the local working copy will not include the latest changes until it has been updated. Editing the newest version of a file is much easier than trying to combine an older, edited local file with the newer version from the repository.

3.5. Reverting Changes

Sometimes it turns out that changes were not necessary after all, or the writer just wants to start over. Files can be "reset" to their unchanged form with svn revert. For example, to erase the edits made to chapter.xml and reset it to unmodified form:

```
% svn revert chapter.xml
```

3.6. Making a Diff

After edits to a file or group of files are completed, the differences between the local working copy and the version on the FreeBSD repository must be collected into a single file for submission. These *diff* files are produced by redirecting the output of svn diff into a file:

```
% cd ~/doc
% svn diff > doc-fix-spelling.diff
```

Give the file a meaningful name that identifies the contents. The example above is for spelling fixes to the whole documentation tree.

If the diff file is to be submitted with the web "Submit a FreeBSD problem report" interface, add a .txt extension to give the earnest and simple-minded web form a clue that the contents are plain text.

Be careful: svn diff includes all changes made in the current directory and any subdirectories. If there are files in the working copy with edits that are not ready to be submitted yet, provide a list of only the files that are to be included:

```
% cd ~/doc
% svn diff disks/chapter.xml printers/chapter.xml    > disks-printers.diff
```

3.7. Subversion References

These examples show very basic usage of Subversion. More detail is available in the Subversion Book and the Subversion documentation.

Chapter 4. Documentation Directory Structure

Files and directories in the `doc/` tree follow a structure meant to:

1. Make it easy to automate converting the document to other formats.

2. Promote consistency between the different documentation organizations, to make it easier to switch between working on different documents.

3. Make it easy to decide where in the tree new documentation should be placed.

In addition, the documentation tree must accommodate documents in many different languages and encodings. It is important that the documentation tree structure does not enforce any particular defaults or cultural preferences.

4.1. The Top Level, `doc/`

There are two types of directory under `doc/`, each with very specific directory names and meanings.

Directory	Usage
`share`	Contains files that are not specific to the various translations and encodings of the documentation. Contains subdirectories to further categorize the information. For example, the files that comprise the make(1) infrastructure are in `share/mk`, while the additional XML support files (such as the FreeBSD extended DocBook DTD) are in `share/xml`.
`lang.encoding`	One directory exists for each available translation and encoding of the documentation, for example `en_US.ISO8859-1/` and `zh_TW.UTF-8/`. The names are long, but by fully specifying the language and encoding we prevent any future headaches when a translation team wants to provide documentation in the same language but in more than one encoding. This also avoids problems that might be caused by a future switch to Unicode.

4.2. The `lang.encoding/` Directories

These directories contain the documents themselves. The documentation is split into up to three more categories at this level, indicated by the different directory names.

Directory	Usage
`articles`	Documentation marked up as a DocBook `article` (or equivalent). Reasonably short, and broken up into sections. Normally only available as one XHTML file.
`books`	Documentation marked up as a DocBook book (or equivalent). Book length, and broken up into chapters. Normally available as both one large XHTML file (for people

Directory	Usage
	with fast connections, or who want to print it easily from a browser) and as a collection of linked, smaller files.
man	For translations of the system manual pages. This directory will contain one or more man*N* directories, corresponding to the sections that have been translated.

Not every *lang* .*encoding* directory will have all of these subdirectories. It depends on how much translation has been accomplished by that translation team.

4.3. Document-Specific Information

This section contains specific notes about particular documents managed by the FDP.

4.3.1. The Handbook

books/handbook/

The Handbook is written in DocBook XML using the FreeBSD DocBook extended DTD.

The Handbook is organized as a DocBook book. The book is divided into parts, each of which contains several chapters. chapters are further subdivided into sections (sect1) and subsections (sect2, sect3) and so on.

4.3.1.1. Physical Organization

There are a number of files and directories within the handbook directory.

> ## Note
>
> The Handbook's organization may change over time, and this document may lag in detailing the organizational changes. Post questions about Handbook organization to the FreeBSD documentation project mailing list.

4.3.1.1.1. Makefile

The Makefile defines some variables that affect how the XML source is converted to other formats, and lists the various source files that make up the Handbook. It then includes the standard doc.project.mk , to bring in the rest of the code that handles converting documents from one format to another.

4.3.1.1.2. book.xml

This is the top level document in the Handbook. It contains the Handbook's DOCTYPE declaration, as well as the elements that describe the Handbook's structure.

book.xml uses parameter entities to load in the files with the .ent extension. These files (described later) then define general entities that are used throughout the rest of the Handbook.

4.3.1.1.3. *directory*/chapter.xml

Each chapter in the Handbook is stored in a file called chapter.xml in a separate directory from the other chapters. Each directory is named after the value of the id attribute on the chapter element.

For example, if one of the chapter files contains:

```
<chapter id="kernelconfig">
```

```
...
</chapter>
```

Then it will be called `chapter.xml` in the `kernelconfig` directory. In general, the entire contents of the chapter are in this one file.

When the XHTML version of the Handbook is produced, this will yield `kernelconfig.html`. This is because of the `id` value, and is not related to the name of the directory.

In earlier versions of the Handbook, the files were stored in the same directory as `book.xml`, and named after the value of the `id` attribute on the file's `chapter` element. Now, it is possible to include images in each chapter. Images for each Handbook chapter are stored within `share/images/books/handbook`. The localized version of these images should be placed in the same directory as the XML sources for each chapter. Namespace collisions are inevitable, and it is easier to work with several directories with a few files in them than it is to work with one directory that has many files in it.

A brief look will show that there are many directories with individual `chapter.xml` files, including `basics/chapter.xml`, `introduction/chapter.xml`, and `printing/chapter.xml`.

Important

Do not name chapters or directories after their ordering within the Handbook. This ordering can change as the content within the Handbook is reorganized. Reorganization should be possible without renaming files, unless entire chapters are being promoted or demoted within the hierarchy.

The `chapter.xml` files are not complete XML documents that can be built individually. They can only be built as parts of the whole Handbook.

Chapter 5. The Documentation Build Process

This chapter covers organization of the documentation build process and how make(1) is used to control it.

5.1. Rendering DocBook into Output

Different types of output can be produced from a single DocBook source file. The type of output desired is set with the FORMATS variable. A list of known formats is stored in KNOWN_FORMATS:

```
% cd ~/doc/en_US.ISO8859-1/books/handbook
% make -V KNOWN_FORMATS
```

Table 5.1. Common Output Formats

FORMATS Value	File Type	Description
html	HTML, one file	A single book.html or article.html.
html-split	HTML, multiple files	Multiple HTML files, one for each chapter or section, for use on a typical web site.
pdf	PDF	Portable Document Format

The default output format can vary by document, but is usually html-split . Other formats are chosen by setting FORMATS to a specific value. Multiple output formats can be created at a single time by setting FORMATS to a list of formats.

Example 5.1. Build a Single HTML Output File

```
% cd ~/doc/en_US.ISO8859-1/books/handbook
% make FORMATS=html
```

Example 5.2. Build HTML-Split and PDF Output Files

```
% cd ~/doc/en_US.ISO8859-1/books/handbook
% make FORMATS="html-split pdf"
```

5.2. The FreeBSD Documentation Build Toolset

These are the tools used to build and install the FDP documentation.

- The primary build tool is make(1), specifically Berkeley Make.

- Package building is handled by FreeBSD's pkg-create(8).

- gzip(1) is used to create compressed versions of the document. bzip2(1) archives are also supported. tar(1) is used for package building.

- install(1) is used to install the documentation.

5.3. Understanding Makefiles in the Documentation Tree

There are three main types of Makefiles in the FreeBSD Documentation Project tree.

- Subdirectory Makefiles simply pass commands to those directories below them.

- Documentation Makefiles describe the documents that are produced from this directory.

- Make includes are the glue that perform the document production, and are usually of the form doc.*xxx*.mk.

5.3.1. Subdirectory Makefiles

These Makefiles usually take the form of:

```
SUBDIR =articles
SUBDIR+=books

COMPAT_SYMLINK = en

DOC_PREFIX?= ${.CURDIR}/..
.include "${DOC_PREFIX}/share/mk/doc.project.mk"
```

The first four non-empty lines define the make(1) variables SUBDIR, COMPAT_SYMLINK, and DOC_PREFIX.

The SUBDIR statement and COMPAT_SYMLINK statement show how to assign a value to a variable, overriding any previous value.

The second SUBDIR statement shows how a value is appended to the current value of a variable. The SUBDIR variable is now articles books.

The DOC_PREFIX assignment shows how a value is assigned to the variable, but only if it is not already defined. This is useful if DOC_PREFIX is not where this Makefile thinks it is - the user can override this and provide the correct value.

What does it all mean? SUBDIR mentions which subdirectories below this one the build process should pass any work on to.

COMPAT_SYMLINK is specific to compatibility symlinks (amazingly enough) for languages to their official encoding (doc/en would point to en_US.ISO-8859-1).

DOC_PREFIX is the path to the root of the FreeBSD Document Project tree. This is not always that easy to find, and is also easily overridden, to allow for flexibility. .CURDIR is a make(1) builtin variable with the path to the current directory.

The final line includes the FreeBSD Documentation Project's project-wide make(1) system file doc.project.mk which is the glue which converts these variables into build instructions.

5.3.2. Documentation Makefiles

These Makefiles set make(1) variables that describe how to build the documentation contained in that directory.

Here is an example:

```
MAINTAINER=nik@FreeBSD.org
```

```
DOC?= book

FORMATS?= html-split html

INSTALL_COMPRESSED?= gz
INSTALL_ONLY_COMPRESSED?=

# SGML content
SRCS=  book.xml

DOC_PREFIX?= ${.CURDIR}/../../..

.include "$(DOC_PREFIX)/share/mk/docproj.docbook.mk"
```

The `MAINTAINER` variable allows committers to claim ownership of a document in the FreeBSD Documentation Project, and take responsibility for maintaining it.

`DOC` is the name (sans the `.xml` extension) of the main document created by this directory. `SRCS` lists all the individual files that make up the document. This should also include important files in which a change should result in a rebuild.

`FORMATS` indicates the default formats that should be built for this document. `INSTALL_COMPRESSED` is the default list of compression techniques that should be used in the document build. `INSTALL_ONLY_COMPRESS`, empty by default, should be non-empty if only compressed documents are desired in the build.

The `DOC_PREFIX` and include statements should be familiar already.

5.4. FreeBSD Documentation Project Make Includes

make(1) includes are best explained by inspection of the code. Here are the system include files:

- `doc.project.mk` is the main project include file, which includes all the following include files, as necessary.

- `doc.subdir.mk` handles traversing of the document tree during the build and install processes.

- `doc.install.mk` provides variables that affect ownership and installation of documents.

- `doc.docbook.mk` is included if `DOCFORMAT` is docbook and `DOC` is set.

5.4.1. `doc.project.mk`

By inspection:

```
DOCFORMAT?= docbook
MAINTAINER?= doc@FreeBSD.org

PREFIX?= /usr/local
PRI_LANG?= en_US.ISO8859-1

.if defined(DOC)
.if ${DOCFORMAT} == "docbook"
.include "doc.docbook.mk"
.endif
.endif

.include "doc.subdir.mk"
.include "doc.install.mk"
```

5.4.1.1. Variables

`DOCFORMAT` and `MAINTAINER` are assigned default values, if these are not set by the document make file.

PREFIX is the prefix under which the documentation building tools are installed. For normal package and port installation, this is /usr/local.

PRI_LANG should be set to whatever language and encoding is natural amongst users these documents are being built for. US English is the default.

Note

PRI_LANG does not affect which documents can, or even will, be built. Its main use is creating links to commonly referenced documents into the FreeBSD documentation install root.

5.4.1.2. Conditionals

The .if defined(DOC) line is an example of a make(1) conditional which, like in other programs, defines behavior if some condition is true or if it is false. defined is a function which returns whether the variable given is defined or not.

.if ${DOCFORMAT} == "docbook", next, tests whether the DOCFORMAT variable is "docbook", and in this case, includes doc.docbook.mk.

The two .endifs close the two above conditionals, marking the end of their application.

5.4.2. doc.subdir.mk

This file is too long to explain in detail. These notes describe the most important features.

5.4.2.1. Variables

- SUBDIR is a list of subdirectories that the build process should go further down into.

- ROOT_SYMLINKS is the name of directories that should be linked to the document install root from their actual locations, if the current language is the primary language (specified by PRI_LANG).

- COMPAT_SYMLINK is described in the Subdirectory Makefile section.

5.4.2.2. Targets and Macros

Dependencies are described by *target: dependency1 dependency2 ...* tuples, where to build target, the given dependencies must be built first.

After that descriptive tuple, instructions on how to build the target may be given, if the conversion process between the target and its dependencies are not previously defined, or if this particular conversion is not the same as the default conversion method.

A special dependency .USE defines the equivalent of a macro.

```
_SUBDIRUSE: .USE
.for entry in ${SUBDIR}
 @${ECHO} "===> ${DIRPRFX}${entry}"
 @(cd ${.CURDIR}/${entry} && \
 ${MAKE} ${.TARGET:S/realpackage/package/:S/realinstall/install/} DIRPRFX=
${DIRPRFX}${entry}/ )
.endfor
```

In the above, _SUBDIRUSE is now a macro which will execute the given commands when it is listed as a dependency.

What sets this macro apart from other targets? Basically, it is executed *after* the instructions given in the build procedure it is listed as a dependency to, and it does not adjust .TARGET, which is the variable which contains the name of the target currently being built.

```
clean: _SUBDIRUSE
 rm -f ${CLEANFILES}
```

In the above, `clean` will use the `_SUBDIRUSE` macro after it has executed the instruction `rm -f ${CLEANFILES}`. In effect, this causes `clean` to go further and further down the directory tree, deleting built files as it goes *down*, not on the way back up.

5.4.2.2.1. Provided Targets

- `install` and `package` both go down the directory tree calling the real versions of themselves in the subdirectories (`realinstall` and `realpackage` respectively).

- `clean` removes files created by the build process (and goes down the directory tree too). `cleandir` does the same, and also removes the object directory, if any.

5.4.2.3. More on Conditionals

- `exists` is another condition function which returns true if the given file exists.

- `empty` returns true if the given variable is empty.

- `target` returns true if the given target does not already exist.

5.4.2.4. Looping Constructs in `make` (`.for`)

`.for` provides a way to repeat a set of instructions for each space-separated element in a variable. It does this by assigning a variable to contain the current element in the list being examined.

```
_SUBDIRUSE: .USE
.for entry in ${SUBDIR}
 @${ECHO} "===> ${DIRPRFX}${entry}"
 @(cd ${.CURDIR}/${entry} && \
 ${MAKE} ${.TARGET:S/realpackage/package/:S/realinstall/install/} DIRPRFX=
${DIRPRFX}${entry}/ )
.endfor
```

In the above, if `SUBDIR` is empty, no action is taken; if it has one or more elements, the instructions between `.for` and `.endfor` would repeat for every element, with `entry` being replaced with the value of the current element.

Chapter 6. The Website

The FreeBSD web site is part of the FreeBSD documents. Files for the web site are stored in the `en_US.ISO8859-1/htdocs` subdirectory of the document tree directory, `~/doc` in this example.

6.1. Environment Variables

Several environment variables control which parts of the web site are built or installed, and to which directories.

> ### Tip
> The web build system uses make(1), and considers variables to be set when they have been defined, even if they are empty. The examples here show the recommended ways of defining and using these variables. Setting or defining these variables with other values or methods might lead to unexpected surprises.

DESTDIR
> DESTDIR specifies the path where the web site files are to be installed.
>
> This variable is best set with env(1) or the user shell's method of setting environment variables, `setenv` for csh(1) or `export` for sh(1).

ENGLISH_ONLY
> Default: undefined. Build and include all translations.
>
> **ENGLISH_ONLY=yes**: use only the English documents and ignore all translations.

WEB_ONLY
> Default: undefined. Build both the web site and all the books and articles.
>
> **WEB_ONLY=yes**: build or install only HTML pages from the `en_US.ISO8859-1/htdocs` directory. Other directories and documents, including books and articles, will be ignored.

WEB_LANG
> Default: undefined. Build and include all the available languages on the web site.
>
> Set to a space-separated list of languages to be included in the build or install. The formats are the same as the directory names in the document root directory. For example, to include the German and French documents:
>
> ```
> WEB_LANG="de_DE.ISO8859-1 fr_FR.ISO8859-1"
> ```

`WEB_ONLY`, `WEB_LANG`, and `ENGLISH_ONLY` are make(1) variables and can be set in `/etc/make.conf`, `Makefile.inc`, as environment variables on the command line, or in dot files.

6.2. Building and Installing the Web Pages

Having obtained the documentation and web site source files, the web site can be built.

An actual installation of the web site is run as the `root` user because the permissions on the web server directory will not allow files to be installed by an unprivileged user. For testing, it can be useful to install the files as a normal user to a temporary directory.

In these examples, the web site files are built by user `jru` in their home directory, `~/doc`, with a full path of `/usr/home/jru/doc`.

Tip

The web site build uses the INDEX from the Ports Collection and might fail if that file or /usr/ports is not present. The simplest approach is to install the Ports Collection.

Example 6.1. Build the Full Web Site and All Documents

Build the web site and all documents. The resulting files are left in the document tree:

```
% cd ~/doc/en_US.ISO8859-1/htdocs/
% make all
```

Example 6.2. Build Only the Web Site in English

Build the web site only, in English, as user jru, and install the resulting files into /tmp/www for testing:

```
% cd ~/doc/en_US.ISO8859-1/htdocs/
% env DESTDIR=/tmp/www make ENGLISH_ONLY=yes WEB_ONLY=yes all install
```

Changes to static files can usually be tested by viewing the modified files directly with a web browser. If the site has been built as shown above, a modified main page can be viewed with:

```
% firefox /tmp/www/data/index.html
```

Modifications to dynamic files can be tested with a web server running on the local system. After building the site as shown above, this /usr/local/etc/apache24/httpd.conf can be used with www/apache24:

```
# httpd.conf for testing the FreeBSD website
Define TestRoot "/tmp/www/data"

# directory for configuration files
ServerRoot "/usr/local"

Listen 80

# minimum required modules
LoadModule authz_core_module libexec/apache24/mod_authz_core.so
LoadModule mime_module libexec/apache24/mod_mime.so
LoadModule unixd_module libexec/apache24/mod_unixd.so
LoadModule cgi_module libexec/apache24/mod_cgi.so
LoadModule dir_module libexec/apache24/mod_dir.so

# run the webserver as user and group
User www
Group www

ServerAdmin you@example.com
ServerName fbsdtest

# deny access to all files
<Directory />
    AllowOverride none
    Require all denied
```

```
    </Directory>

    # allow access to the website directory
    DocumentRoot "${TestRoot}"
    <Directory "${TestRoot}">
        Options Indexes FollowSymLinks
        AllowOverride None
        Require all granted
    </Directory>

    # prevent access to .htaccess and .htpasswd files
    <Files ".ht*">
        Require all denied
    </Files>

    ErrorLog "/var/log/httpd-error.log"
    LogLevel warn

    # set up the CGI script directory
    <Directory "${TestRoot}/cgi">
        AllowOverride None
        Options None
        Require all granted
        Options +ExecCGI
        AddHandler cgi-script .cgi
    </Directory>

    Include etc/apache24/Includes/*.conf
```

Start the web server with

```
# service apache24 onestart
```

The web site can be viewed at http://localhost. Be aware that many links refer to the real FreeBSD site by name, and those links will still go to the external site instead of the local test version. Fully testing the local site will require temporarily setting DNS so www.FreeBSD.org resolves to localhost or the local IP address.

Example 6.3. Build and Install the Web Site

Build the web site and all documents as user jru. Install the resulting files as root into the default directory, /root/public_html:

```
% cd ~/doc/en_US.ISO8859-1/htdocs
% make all
% su -
Password:
# cd /usr/home/jru/doc/en_US.ISO8859-1/htdocs
# make install
```

The install process does not delete any old or outdated files that existed previously in the same directory. If a new copy of the site is built and installed every day, this command will find and delete all files that have not been updated in three days:

```
# find /usr/local/www -ctime 3 -delete
```

Chapter 7. XML Primer

Most FDP documentation is written with markup languages based on XML. This chapter explains what that means, how to read and understand the documentation source, and the XML techniques used.

Portions of this section were inspired by Mark Galassi's Get Going With DocBook.

7.1. Overview

In the original days of computers, electronic text was simple. There were a few character sets like ASCII or EBCDIC, but that was about it. Text was text, and what you saw really was what you got. No frills, no formatting, no intelligence.

Inevitably, this was not enough. When text is in a machine-usable format, machines are expected to be able to use and manipulate it intelligently. Authors want to indicate that certain phrases should be emphasized, or added to a glossary, or made into hyperlinks. Filenames could be shown in a "typewriter" style font for viewing on screen, but as "italics" when printed, or any of a myriad of other options for presentation.

It was once hoped that Artificial Intelligence (AI) would make this easy. The computer would read the document and automatically identify key phrases, filenames, text that the reader should type in, examples, and more. Unfortunately, real life has not happened quite like that, and computers still require assistance before they can meaningfully process text.

More precisely, they need help identifying what is what. Consider this text:

To remove `/tmp/foo` , use rm(1).

```
% rm /tmp/foo
```

It is easy to see which parts are filenames, which are commands to be typed in, which parts are references to manual pages, and so on. But the computer processing the document cannot. For this we need markup.

"Markup" is commonly used to describe "adding value" or "increasing cost". The term takes on both these meanings when applied to text. Markup is additional text included in the document, distinguished from the document's content in some way, so that programs that process the document can read the markup and use it when making decisions about the document. Editors can hide the markup from the user, so the user is not distracted by it.

The extra information stored in the markup *adds value* to the document. Adding the markup to the document must typically be done by a person—after all, if computers could recognize the text sufficiently well to add the markup then there would be no need to add it in the first place. This *increases the cost* (the effort required) to create the document.

The previous example is actually represented in this document like this:

```
<para>To remove <filename>/tmp/foo</filename> , use &man.rm.1;.</para>

<screen>&prompt.user; <userinput> rm /tmp/foo</userinput> </screen>
```

The markup is clearly separate from the content.

Markup languages define what the markup means and how it should be interpreted.

Of course, one markup language might not be enough. A markup language for technical documentation has very different requirements than a markup language that is intended for cookery recipes. This, in turn, would be very different from a markup language used to describe poetry. What is really needed is a first language used to write these other markup languages. A *meta markup language*.

This is exactly what the eXtensible Markup Language (XML) is. Many markup languages have been written in XML, including the two most used by the FDP, XHTML and DocBook.

Each language definition is more properly called a grammar, vocabulary, schema or Document Type Definition (DTD). There are various languages to specify an XML grammar, or *schema*.

A schema is a *complete* specification of all the elements that are allowed to appear, the order in which they should appear, which elements are mandatory, which are optional, and so forth. This makes it possible to write an XML *parser* which reads in both the schema and a document which claims to conform to the schema. The parser can then confirm whether or not all the elements required by the vocabulary are in the document in the right order, and whether there are any errors in the markup. This is normally referred to as "validating the document".

Note

Validation confirms that the choice of elements, their ordering, and so on, conforms to that listed in the grammar. It does *not* check whether *appropriate* markup has been used for the content. If all the filenames in a document were marked up as function names, the parser would not flag this as an error (assuming, of course, that the schema defines elements for filenames and functions, and that they are allowed to appear in the same place).

Most contributions to the Documentation Project will be content marked up in either XHTML or DocBook, rather than alterations to the schemas. For this reason, this book will not touch on how to write a vocabulary.

7.2. Elements, Tags, and Attributes

All the vocabularies written in XML share certain characteristics. This is hardly surprising, as the philosophy behind XML will inevitably show through. One of the most obvious manifestations of this philosophy is that of *content* and *elements*.

Documentation, whether it is a single web page, or a lengthy book, is considered to consist of content. This content is then divided and further subdivided into elements. The purpose of adding markup is to name and identify the boundaries of these elements for further processing.

For example, consider a typical book. At the very top level, the book is itself an element. This "book" element obviously contains chapters, which can be considered to be elements in their own right. Each chapter will contain more elements, such as paragraphs, quotations, and footnotes. Each paragraph might contain further elements, identifying content that was direct speech, or the name of a character in the story.

It may be helpful to think of this as "chunking" content. At the very top level is one chunk, the book. Look a little deeper, and there are more chunks, the individual chapters. These are chunked further into paragraphs, footnotes, character names, and so on.

Notice how this differentiation between different elements of the content can be made without resorting to any XML terms. It really is surprisingly straightforward. This could be done with a highlighter pen and a printout of the book, using different colors to indicate different chunks of content.

Of course, we do not have an electronic highlighter pen, so we need some other way of indicating which element each piece of content belongs to. In languages written in XML (XHTML, DocBook, et al) this is done by means of *tags*.

A tag is used to identify where a particular element starts, and where the element ends. *The tag is not part of the element itself*. Because each grammar was normally written to mark up specific types of information, each one will recognize different elements, and will therefore have different names for the tags.

For an element called `element-name` the start tag will normally look like `<element-name>`. The corresponding closing tag for this element is `</element-name>`.

Example 7.1. Using an Element (Start and End Tags)

XHTML has an element for indicating that the content enclosed by the element is a paragraph, called p.

```
<p>This is a paragraph.  It starts with the start tag for
  the 'p' element, and it will end with the end tag for the 'p'
  element.</p>

<p>This is another paragraph.  But this one is much shorter.</p>
```

Some elements have no content. For example, in XHTML, a horizontal line can be included in the document. For these "empty" elements, XML introduced a shorthand form that is completely equivalent to the two-tag version:

Example 7.2. Using an Element Without Content

XHTML has an element for indicating a horizontal rule, called hr. This element does not wrap content, so it looks like this:

```
<p>One paragraph.</p>
<hr></hr>

<p>This is another paragraph.  A horizontal rule separates this
  from the previous paragraph.</p>
```

The shorthand version consists of a single tag:

```
<p>One paragraph.</p>
<hr/>

<p>This is another paragraph.  A horizontal rule separates this
  from the previous paragraph.</p>
```

As shown above, elements can contain other elements. In the book example earlier, the book element contained all the chapter elements, which in turn contained all the paragraph elements, and so on.

Example 7.3. Elements Within Elements; em

```
<p>This is a simple <em>paragraph</em> where some
  of the <em>words</em> have been <em>emphasized</em>.</p>
```

The grammar consists of rules that describe which elements can contain other elements, and exactly what they can contain.

Important

People often confuse the terms tags and elements, and use the terms as if they were interchangeable. They are not.

> An element is a conceptual part of your document. An element has a defined start and end. The tags mark where the element starts and ends.
>
> When this document (or anyone else knowledgeable about XML) refers to "the <p> tag" they mean the literal text consisting of the three characters <, p, and >. But the phrase "the p element" refers to the whole element.
>
> This distinction *is* very subtle. But keep it in mind.

Elements can have attributes. An attribute has a name and a value, and is used for adding extra information to the element. This might be information that indicates how the content should be rendered, or might be something that uniquely identifies that occurrence of the element, or it might be something else.

An element's attributes are written *inside* the start tag for that element, and take the form `attribute-name="attribute-value"`.

In XHTML, the p element has an attribute called `align`, which suggests an alignment (justification) for the paragraph to the program displaying the XHTML.

The `align` attribute can take one of four defined values, `left`, `center`, `right` and `justify`. If the attribute is not specified then the default is `left`.

Example 7.4. Using an Element with an Attribute

```
<p align="left"> The inclusion of the align attribute
  on this paragraph was superfluous, since the default is left.</p>

<p align="center"> This may appear in the center.</p>
```

Some attributes only take specific values, such as `left` or `justify`. Others allow any value.

Example 7.5. Single Quotes Around Attributes

```
<p align='right'> I am on the right!</p>
```

Attribute values in XML must be enclosed in either single or double quotes. Double quotes are traditional. Single quotes are useful when the attribute value contains double quotes.

Information about attributes, elements, and tags is stored in catalog files. The Documentation Project uses standard DocBook catalogs and includes additional catalogs for FreeBSD-specific features. Paths to the catalog files are defined in an environment variable so they can be found by the document build tools.

7.2.1. To Do...

Before running the examples in this document, install textproc/docproj from the FreeBSD Ports Collection. This is a *meta-port* that downloads and installs the standard programs and supporting files needed by the Documentation Project. csh(1) users must use `rehash` for the shell to recognize new programs after they have been installed, or log out and then log back in again.

1. Create `example.xml`, and enter this text:

```
<!DOCTYPE html PUBLIC "-//W3C//DTD XHTML 1.0 Transitional//EN" "http://www.w3.org/TR/
xhtml1/DTD/xhtml1-transitional.dtd">

<html xmlns="http://www.w3.org/1999/xhtml">
  <head>
    <title>An Example XHTML File</title>
  </head>

  <body>
    <p>This is a paragraph containing some text.</p>

    <p>This paragraph contains some more text.</p>

    <p align="right"> This paragraph might be right-justified.</p>
  </body>
</html>
```

2.   Try to validate this file using an XML parser.

     textproc/docproj includes the xmllint validating parser [22].

     Use xmllint to validate the document:

```
% xmllint --valid --noout example.xml
```

     xmllint returns without displaying any output, showing that the document validated successfully.

3.   See what happens when required elements are omitted. Delete the line with the `<title>` and `</title>` tags,
     and re-run the validation.

```
% xmllint --valid --noout example.xml
example.xml:5: element head: validity error : Element head content does not follow ↺
the DTD, expecting ((script | style | meta | link | object | isindex)* , ((title , ↺
(script | style | meta | link | object | isindex)* , (base , (script | style | meta
 | link | object | isindex)*)?) | (base , (script | style | meta | link | object | ↺
isindex)* , title , (script | style | meta | link | object | isindex)*))), got ()
```

     This shows that the validation error comes from the *fifth* line of the *example.xml* file and that the content
     of the `<head>` is the part which does not follow the rules of the XHTML grammar.

     Then xmllint shows the line where the error was found and marks the exact character position with a ^ sign.

4.   Replace the title element.

7.3. The DOCTYPE Declaration

The beginning of each document can specify the name of the DTD to which the document conforms. This DOCTYPE
declaration is used by XML parsers to identify the DTD and ensure that the document does conform to it.

A typical declaration for a document written to conform with version 1.0 of the XHTML DTD looks like this:

```
<!DOCTYPE html PUBLIC "-//W3C//DTD XHTML 1.0 Transitional//EN" "http://www.w3.org/TR/
xhtml1/DTD/xhtml1-transitional.dtd">
```

That line contains a number of different components.

`<!`
     The *indicator* shows this is an XML declaration.

`DOCTYPE`
     Shows that this is an XML declaration of the document type.

25

`html`

Names the first element that will appear in the document.

`PUBLIC "-//W3C//DTD XHTML 1.0 Transitional//EN"`

Lists the Formal Public Identifier (FPI) for the DTD to which this document conforms. The XML parser uses this to find the correct DTD when processing this document.

PUBLIC is not a part of the FPI, but indicates to the XML processor how to find the DTD referenced in the FPI. Other ways of telling the XML parser how to find the DTD are shown later.

`"http://www.w3.org/TR/xhtml1/DTD/xhtml1-transitional.dtd"`

A local filename or a URL to find the DTD.

`>`

Ends the declaration and returns to the document.

7.3.1. Formal Public Identifiers (FPIs)

Note

It is not necessary to know this, but it is useful background, and might help debug problems when the XML processor can not locate the DTD.

FPIs must follow a specific syntax:

`"Owner//Keyword Description //Language "`

`Owner`

The owner of the FPI.

The beginning of the string identifies the owner of the FPI. For example, the FPI `"ISO 8879:1986//ENTITIES Greek Symbols//EN"` lists `ISO 8879:1986` as being the owner for the set of entities for Greek symbols. ISO 8879:1986 is the International Organization for Standardization (ISO) number for the SGML standard, the predecessor (and a superset) of XML.

Otherwise, this string will either look like `-//Owner` or `+//Owner` (notice the only difference is the leading + or -).

If the string starts with - then the owner information is unregistered, with a + identifying it as registered.

ISO 9070:1991 defines how registered names are generated. It might be derived from the number of an ISO publication, an ISBN code, or an organization code assigned according to ISO 6523. Additionally, a registration authority could be created in order to assign registered names. The ISO council delegated this to the American National Standards Institute (ANSI).

Because the FreeBSD Project has not been registered, the owner string is `-//FreeBSD`. As seen in the example, the W3C are not a registered owner either.

`Keyword`

There are several keywords that indicate the type of information in the file. Some of the most common keywords are DTD, ELEMENT, ENTITIES, and TEXT. DTD is used only for DTD files, ELEMENT is usually used for DTD fragments that contain only entity or element declarations. TEXT is used for XML content (text and tags).

`Description`

Any description can be given for the contents of this file. This may include version numbers or any short text that is meaningful and unique for the XML system.

Language
> An ISO two-character code that identifies the native language for the file. EN is used for English.

7.3.1.1. catalog Files

With the syntax above, an XML processor needs to have some way of turning the FPI into the name of the file containing the DTD. A catalog file (typically called `catalog`) contains lines that map FPIs to filenames. For example, if the catalog file contained the line:

```
PUBLIC  "-//W3C//DTD XHTML 1.0 Transitional//EN"        "1.0/transitional.dtd"
```

The XML processor knows that the DTD is called `transitional.dtd` in the `1.0` subdirectory of the directory that held `catalog`.

Examine the contents of `/usr/local/share/xml/dtd/xhtml/catalog.xml` . This is the catalog file for the XHTML DTDs that were installed as part of the textproc/docproj port.

7.3.2. Alternatives to FPIs

Instead of using an FPI to indicate the DTD to which the document conforms (and therefore, which file on the system contains the DTD), the filename can be explicitly specified.

The syntax is slightly different:

```
<!DOCTYPE html SYSTEM "/path/to/file.dtd">
```

The `SYSTEM` keyword indicates that the XML processor should locate the DTD in a system specific fashion. This typically (but not always) means the DTD will be provided as a filename.

Using FPIs is preferred for reasons of portability. If the `SYSTEM` identifier is used, then the DTD must be provided and kept in the same location for everyone.

7.4. Escaping Back to XML

Some of the underlying XML syntax can be useful within documents. For example, comments can be included in the document, and will be ignored by the parser. Comments are entered using XML syntax. Other uses for XML syntax will be shown later.

XML sections begin with a <! tag and end with a >. These sections contain instructions for the parser rather than elements of the document. Everything between these tags is XML syntax. The DOCTYPE declaration shown earlier is an example of XML syntax included in the document.

7.5. Comments

An XML document may contain comments. They may appear anywhere as long as they are not inside tags. They are even allowed in some locations inside the DTD (e.g., between entity declarations).

XML comments start with the string "`<!--`" and end with the string "`-->`".

Here are some examples of valid XML comments:

Example 7.6. XML Generic Comments

```
<!-- This is inside the comment -->
```

```
<!--This is another comment-->

<!-- This is how you
     write multiline comments -->

<p>A simple <!-- Comment inside an element's content --> paragraph.</p>
```

XML comments may contain any strings except "--":

Example 7.7. Erroneous XML Comment

```
<!-- This comment--is wrong -->
```

7.5.1. To Do...

1. Add some comments to `example.xml`, and check that the file still validates using `xmllint`.

2. Add some invalid comments to `example.xml`, and see the error messages that `xmllint` gives when it encounters an invalid comment.

7.6. Entities

Entities are a mechanism for assigning names to chunks of content. As an XML parser processes a document, any entities it finds are replaced by the content of the entity.

This is a good way to have re-usable, easily changeable chunks of content in XML documents. It is also the only way to include one marked up file inside another using XML.

There are two types of entities for two different situations: *general entities* and *parameter entities*.

7.6.1. General Entities

General entities are used to assign names to reusable chunks of text. These entities can only be used in the document. They cannot be used in an XML context.

To include the text of a general entity in the document, include *&entity-name*; in the text. For example, consider a general entity called `current.version` which expands to the current version number of a product. To use it in the document, write:

```
<para>The current version of our product is
  &current.version;.</para>
```

When the version number changes, edit the definition of the general entity, replacing the value. Then reprocess the document.

General entities can also be used to enter characters that could not otherwise be included in an XML document. For example, < and & cannot normally appear in an XML document. The XML parser sees the < symbol as the start of a tag. Likewise, when the & symbol is seen, the next text is expected to be an entity name.

These symbols can be included by using two predefined general entities: < and &.

General entities can only be defined within an XML context. Such definitions are usually done immediately after the DOCTYPE declaration.

Example 7.8. Defining General Entities

```
<!DOCTYPE html PUBLIC "-//W3C//DTD XHTML 1.0 Transitional//EN"
"http://www.w3.org/TR/xhtml1/DTD/xhtml1-transitional.dtd" [
<!ENTITY current.version    "3.0-RELEASE">
<!ENTITY last.version       "2.2.7-RELEASE">
]>
```

The DOCTYPE declaration has been extended by adding a square bracket at the end of the first line. The two entities are then defined over the next two lines, the square bracket is closed, and then the DOCTYPE declaration is closed.

The square brackets are necessary to indicate that the DTD indicated by the DOCTYPE declaration is being extended.

7.6.2. Parameter Entities

Parameter entities, like general entities, are used to assign names to reusable chunks of text. But parameter entities can only be used within an XML context.

Parameter entity definitions are similar to those for general entities. However, parameter entries are included with %*entity-name* ;. The definition also includes the % between the ENTITY keyword and the name of the entity.

For a mnemonic, think "*Parameter* entities use the *Percent* symbol".

Example 7.9. Defining Parameter Entities

```
<!DOCTYPE html PUBLIC "-//W3C//DTD XHTML 1.0 Transitional//EN"
"http://www.w3.org/TR/xhtml1/DTD/xhtml1-transitional.dtd" [
<!ENTITY % param.some "some">
<!ENTITY % param.text "text">
<!ENTITY % param.new  "%param.some more %param.text">

<!-- %param.new now contains "some more text" -->
]>
```

7.6.3. To Do...

1. Add a general entity to example.xml.

    ```
    <!DOCTYPE html PUBLIC "-//W3C//DTD XHTML 1.0 Transitional//EN"
    "http://www.w3.org/TR/xhtml1/DTD/xhtml1-transitional.dtd" [
    <!ENTITY version "1.1">
    ]>

    <html xmlns="http://www.w3.org/1999/xhtml">
      <head>
        <title>An Example XHTML File</title>
      </head>

      <!-- There may be some comments in here as well -->
    ```

```
<body>
  <p>This is a paragraph containing some text.</p>

  <p>This paragraph contains some more text.</p>

  <p align="right"> This paragraph might be right-justified.</p>

  <p>The current version of this document is: &version;</p>
</body>
</html>
```

2. Validate the document using xmllint.

3. Load example.xml into a web browser. It may have to be copied to example.html before the browser recognizes it as an XHTML document.

    Older browsers with simple parsers may not render this file as expected. The entity reference &version; may not be replaced by the version number, or the XML context closing]> may not be recognized and instead shown in the output.

4. The solution is to *normalize* the document with an XML normalizer. The normalizer reads valid XML and writes equally valid XML which has been transformed in some way. One way the normalizer transforms the input is by expanding all the entity references in the document, replacing the entities with the text that they represent.

    xmllint can be used for this. It also has an option to drop the initial DTD section so that the closing]> does not confuse browsers:

    ```
    % xmllint --noent --dropdtd example.xml > example.html
    ```

    A normalized copy of the document with entities expanded is produced in example.html, ready to load into a web browser.

7.7. Using Entities to Include Files

Both general and parameter entities are particularly useful for including one file inside another.

7.7.1. Using General Entities to Include Files

Consider some content for an XML book organized into files, one file per chapter, called chapter1.xml, chapter2.xml, and so forth, with a book.xml that will contain these chapters.

In order to use the contents of these files as the values for entities, they are declared with the SYSTEM keyword. This directs the XML parser to include the contents of the named file as the value of the entity.

Example 7.10. Using General Entities to Include Files

```
<!DOCTYPE html PUBLIC "-//W3C//DTD XHTML 1.0 Transitional//EN"
"http://www.w3.org/TR/xhtml1/DTD/xhtml1-transitional.dtd" [
<!ENTITY chapter.1 SYSTEM "chapter1.xml">
<!ENTITY chapter.2 SYSTEM "chapter2.xml">
<!ENTITY chapter.3 SYSTEM "chapter3.xml">
<!-- And so forth -->
]>

<html xmlns="http://www.w3.org/1999/xhtml">
  <!-- Use the entities to load in the chapters -->
```

```
   &chapter.1;
   &chapter.2;
   &chapter.3;
</html>
```

 Warning

When using general entities to include other files within a document, the files being included (chapter1.xml, chapter2.xml, and so on) *must not* start with a DOCTYPE declaration. This is a syntax error because entities are low-level constructs and they are resolved before any parsing happens.

7.7.2. Using Parameter Entities to Include Files

Parameter entities can only be used inside an XML context. Including a file in an XML context can be used to ensure that general entities are reusable.

Suppose that there are many chapters in the document, and these chapters were reused in two different books, each book organizing the chapters in a different fashion.

The entities could be listed at the top of each book, but that quickly becomes cumbersome to manage.

Instead, place the general entity definitions inside one file, and use a parameter entity to include that file within the document.

Example 7.11. Using Parameter Entities to Include Files

Place the entity definitions in a separate file called chapters.ent and containing this text:

```
<!ENTITY chapter.1 SYSTEM "chapter1.xml">
<!ENTITY chapter.2 SYSTEM "chapter2.xml">
<!ENTITY chapter.3 SYSTEM "chapter3.xml">
```

Create a parameter entity to refer to the contents of the file. Then use the parameter entity to load the file into the document, which will then make all the general entities available for use. Then use the general entities as before:

```
<!DOCTYPE html PUBLIC "-//W3C//DTD XHTML 1.0 Transitional//EN"
"http://www.w3.org/TR/xhtml1/DTD/xhtml1-transitional.dtd" [
<!-- Define a parameter entity to load in the chapter general entities -->
<!ENTITY % chapters SYSTEM "chapters.ent">

<!-- Now use the parameter entity to load in this file -->
%chapters;
]>

<html xmlns="http://www.w3.org/1999/xhtml">
   &chapter.1;
   &chapter.2;
   &chapter.3;
</html>
```

7.7.3. To Do...

7.7.3.1. Use General Entities to Include Files

1. Create three files, `para1.xml`, `para2.xml`, and `para3.xml`.

    Put content like this in each file:

    ```
    <p>This is the first paragraph.</p>
    ```

2. Edit `example.xml` so that it looks like this:

    ```
    <!DOCTYPE html PUBLIC "-//W3C//DTD XHTML 1.0 Transitional//EN"
    "http://www.w3.org/TR/xhtml1/DTD/xhtml1-transitional.dtd" [
    <!ENTITY version "1.1">
    <!ENTITY para1 SYSTEM "para1.xml">
    <!ENTITY para2 SYSTEM "para2.xml">
    <!ENTITY para3 SYSTEM "para3.xml">
    ]>

    <html xmlns="http://www.w3.org/1999/xhtml">
      <head>
        <title>An Example XHTML File</title>
      </head>

      <body>
        <p>The current version of this document is: &version;</p>

        &para1;
        &para2;
        &para3;
      </body>
    </html>
    ```

3. Produce `example.html` by normalizing `example.xml`.

    ```
    % xmllint --dropdtd --noent example.xml > example.html
    ```

4. Load `example.html` into the web browser and confirm that the `paran.xml` files have been included in `example.html`.

7.7.3.2. Use Parameter Entities to Include Files

 Note

The previous steps must have completed before this step.

1. Edit `example.xml` so that it looks like this:

    ```
    <!DOCTYPE html PUBLIC "-//W3C//DTD XHTML 1.0 Transitional//EN"
    "http://www.w3.org/TR/xhtml1/DTD/xhtml1-transitional.dtd" [
    <!ENTITY % entities SYSTEM "entities.ent"> %entities;
    ]>

    <html xmlns="http://www.w3.org/1999/xhtml">
      <head>
        <title>An Example XHTML File</title>
      </head>

      <body>
        <p>The current version of this document is: &version;</p>
    ```

```
      &para1;
      &para2;
      &para3;
  </body>
</html>
```

2. Create a new file called `entities.ent` with this content:

```
<!ENTITY version "1.1">
<!ENTITY para1 SYSTEM "para1.xml">
<!ENTITY para2 SYSTEM "para2.xml">
<!ENTITY para3 SYSTEM "para3.xml">
```

3. Produce `example.html` by normalizing `example.xml`.

```
% xmllint --dropdtd --noent example.xml > example.html
```

4. Load `example.html` into the web browser and confirm that the `paran.xml` files have been included in `example.html`.

7.8. Marked Sections

XML provides a mechanism to indicate that particular pieces of the document should be processed in a special way. These are called "marked sections".

Example 7.12. Structure of a Marked Section

```
<![KEYWORD [
  Contents of marked section
]]>
```

As expected of an XML construct, a marked section starts with `<!`.

The first square bracket begins the marked section.

KEYWORD describes how this marked section is to be processed by the parser.

The second square bracket indicates the start of the marked section's content.

The marked section is finished by closing the two square brackets, and then returning to the document context from the XML context with `>`.

7.8.1. Marked Section Keywords

7.8.1.1. CDATA

These keywords denote the marked sections *content model*, and allow you to change it from the default.

When an XML parser is processing a document, it keeps track of the "content model".

The content model describes the content the parser is expecting to see and what it will do with that content.

The CDATA content model is one of the most useful.

CDATA is for "Character Data". When the parser is in this content model, it expects to see only characters. In this model the < and & symbols lose their special status, and will be treated as ordinary characters.

Note

When using CDATA in examples of text marked up in XML, remember that the content of CDATA is not validated. The included text must be check with other means. For example, the content could be written in another document, validated, and then pasted into the CDATA section.

Example 7.13. Using a CDATA Marked Section

```
<para>Here is an example of how to include some text that contains
  many <literal>&lt;</literal> and <literal>&amp;</literal>
  symbols.  The sample text is a fragment of
  <acronym>XHTML</acronym>.  The surrounding text (<para> and
  <programlisting> ) are from DocBook.</para>

<programlisting> <![CDATA[<p>This is a sample that shows some of the
  elements within <acronym>XHTML</acronym>.  Since the angle
  brackets are used so many times, it is simpler to say the whole
  example is a CDATA marked section than to use the entity names for
  the left and right angle brackets throughout.</p>

  <ul>
    <li>This is a listitem</li>
    <li>This is a second listitem</li>
    <li>This is a third listitem</li>
  </ul>

  <p>This is the end of the example.</p>]]></programlisting>
```

7.8.1.2. INCLUDE and IGNORE

When the keyword is INCLUDE, then the contents of the marked section will be processed. When the keyword is IGNORE, the marked section is ignored and will not be processed. It will not appear in the output.

Example 7.14. Using INCLUDE and IGNORE in Marked Sections

```
<![INCLUDE[
  This text will be processed and included.
]]>

<![IGNORE[
  This text will not be processed or included.
]]>
```

By itself, this is not too useful. Text to be removed from the document could be cut out, or wrapped in comments.

It becomes more useful when controlled by parameter entities, yet this usage is limited to entity files.

For example, suppose that documentation was produced in a hard-copy version and an electronic version. Some extra text is desired in the electronic version content that was not to appear in the hard-copy.

Create an entity file that defines general entities to include each chapter and guard these definitions with a parameter entity that can be set to either `INCLUDE` or `IGNORE` to control whether the entity is defined. After these conditional general entity definitions, place one more definition for each general entity to set them to an empty value. This technique makes use of the fact that entity definitions cannot be overridden but the first definition always takes effect. So the inclusion of the chapter is controlled with the corresponding parameter entity. Set to `INCLUDE`, the first general entity definition will be read and the second one will be ignored. Set to `IGNORE`, the first definition will be ignored and the second one will take effect.

Example 7.15. Using a Parameter Entity to Control a Marked Section

```
<!ENTITY % electronic.copy "INCLUDE">

<![%electronic.copy;[
<!ENTITY chap.preface SYSTEM "preface.xml">
]]>

<!ENTITY chap.preface "">
```

When producing the hard-copy version, change the parameter entity's definition to:

```
<!ENTITY % electronic.copy "IGNORE">
```

7.8.2. To Do...

1. Modify `entities.ent` to contain the following:

   ```
   <!ENTITY version "1.1">
   <!ENTITY % conditional.text "IGNORE">

   <![%conditional.text;[
   <!ENTITY para1 SYSTEM "para1.xml">
   ]]>

   <!ENTITY para1 "">

   <!ENTITY para2 SYSTEM "para2.xml">
   <!ENTITY para3 SYSTEM "para3.xml">
   ```

2. Normalize `example.xml` and notice that the conditional text is not present in the output document. Set the parameter entity guard to `INCLUDE` and regenerate the normalized document and the text will appear again. This method makes sense if there are more conditional chunks depending on the same condition. For example, to control generating printed or online text.

7.9. Conclusion

That is the conclusion of this XML primer. For reasons of space and complexity, several things have not been covered in depth (or at all). However, the previous sections cover enough XML to introduce the organization of the FDP documentation.

Chapter 8. XHTML Markup

8.1. Introduction

This chapter describes usage of the XHTML markup language used for the FreeBSD web site.

XHTML is the XML version of the HyperText Markup Language, the markup language of choice on the World Wide Web. More information can be found at http://www.w3.org/ .

XHTML is used to mark up pages on the FreeBSD web site. It is usually not used to mark up other documentation, since DocBook offers a far richer set of elements from which to choose. Consequently, XHTML pages will normally only be encountered when writing for the web site.

HTML has gone through a number of versions. The XML-compliant version described here is called XHTML. The latest widespread version is XHTML 1.0, available in both *strict* and *transitional* variants.

The XHTML DTDs are available from the Ports Collection in textproc/xhtml. They are automatically installed by the textproc/docproj port.

Note

This is *not* an exhaustive list of elements, since that would just repeat the documentation for XHTML. The aim is to list those elements most commonly used. Please post questions about elements or uses not covered here to the FreeBSD documentation project mailing list.

Inline Versus Block

In the remainder of this document, when describing elements, *inline* means that the element can occur within a block element, and does not cause a line break. A *block* element, by comparison, will cause a line break (and other processing) when it is encountered.

8.2. Formal Public Identifier (FPI)

There are a number of XHTML FPIs, depending upon the version, or *level* of XHTML to which a document conforms. Most XHTML documents on the FreeBSD web site comply with the transitional version of XHTML 1.0.

```
PUBLIC "-//W3C//DTD XHTML 1.0 Transitional//EN"
```

8.3. Sectional Elements

An XHTML document is normally split into two sections. The first section, called the *head*, contains meta-information about the document, such as its title, the name of the author, the parent document, and so on. The second section, the *body*, contains content that will be displayed to the user.

These sections are indicated with head and body elements respectively. These elements are contained within the top-level html element.

Example 8.1. Normal XHTML Document Structure

```
<html xmlns="http://www.w3.org/1999/xhtml">
  <head>
   <title> The Document's Title </title>
  </head>

  <body>

    ...

  </body>
</html>
```

8.4. Block Elements

8.4.1. Headings

XHTML has tags to denote headings in the document at up to six different levels.

The largest and most prominent heading is h1, then h2, continuing down to h6.

The element's content is the text of the heading.

Example 8.2. h1, h2, and Other Header Tags

Usage:

```
<h1>First section</h1>

<!-- Document introduction goes here -->

<h2>This is the heading for the first section</h2>

<!-- Content for the first section goes here -->

<h3>This is the heading for the first sub-section</h3>

<!-- Content for the first sub-section goes here -->

<h2>This is the heading for the second section</h2>

<!-- Content for the second section goes here -->
```

Generally, an XHTML page should have one first level heading (h1). This can contain many second level headings (h2), which can in turn contain many third level headings. Do not leave gaps in the numbering.

8.4.2. Paragraphs

XHTML supports a single paragraph element, p.

Example 8.3. p Example

Usage:

```
<p>This is a paragraph.  It can contain just about any
  other element.</p>
```

8.4.3. Block Quotations

A block quotation is an extended quotation from another document that will appear in a separate paragraph.

Example 8.4. blockquote Example

Usage:

```
<p>A small excerpt from the US Constitution:</p>

<blockquote> We the People of the United States, in Order to form
  a more perfect Union, establish Justice, insure domestic
  Tranquility, provide for the common defence, promote the general
  Welfare, and secure the Blessings of Liberty to ourselves and our
  Posterity, do ordain and establish this Constitution for the
  United States of America.</blockquote>
```

8.4.4. Lists

XHTML can present the user with three types of lists: ordered, unordered, and definition.

Entries in an ordered list will be numbered, while entries in an unordered list will be preceded by bullet points. Definition lists have two sections for each entry. The first section is the term being defined, and the second section is the definition.

Ordered lists are indicated by the ol element, unordered lists by the ul element, and definition lists by the dl element.

Ordered and unordered lists contain listitems, indicated by the li element. A listitem can contain textual content, or it may be further wrapped in one or more p elements.

Definition lists contain definition terms (dt) and definition descriptions (dd). A definition term can only contain inline elements. A definition description can contain other block elements.

Example 8.5. ul and ol Example

Usage:

```
<p>An unordered list.  Listitems will probably be
  preceded by bullets.</p>

<ul>
```

```
    <li>First item</li>

    <li>Second item</li>

    <li>Third item</li>
</ul>

<p>An ordered list, with list items consisting of multiple
  paragraphs.  Each item (note: not each paragraph) will be
  numbered.</p>

<ol>
  <li><p>This is the first item.  It only has one paragraph.</p></li>

  <li><p>This is the first paragraph of the second item.</p>

    <p>This is the second paragraph of the second item.</p></li>

  <li><p>This is the first and only paragraph of the third
    item.</p></li>
</ol>
```

Example 8.6. Definition Lists with dl

Usage:

```
<dl>
  <dt>Term 1</dt>

  <dd><p>Paragraph 1 of definition 1.</p>

    <p>Paragraph 2 of definition 1.</p></dd>

  <dt>Term 2</dt>

  <dd><p>Paragraph 1 of definition 2.</p></dd>

  <dt>Term 3</dt>

  <dd><p>Paragraph 1 of definition 3.</p></dd>
</dl>
```

8.4.5. Pre-formatted Text

Pre-formatted text is shown to the user exactly as it is in the file. Text is shown in a fixed font. Multiple spaces and line breaks are shown exactly as they are in the file.

Wrap pre-formatted text in the pre element.

Example 8.7. pre Example

For example, the pre tags could be used to mark up an email message:

```
<pre>  From: nik@FreeBSD.org
  To: freebsd-doc@FreeBSD.org
```

```
Subject: New documentation available

There is a new copy of my primer for contributors to the FreeBSD
Documentation Project available at

  &lt;URL:https://people.FreeBSD.org/~nik/primer/index.html&gt;

Comments appreciated.

N</pre>
```

Keep in mind that < and & still are recognized as special characters in pre-formatted text. This is why the example shown had to use < instead of <. For consistency, > was used in place of >, too. Watch out for the special characters that may appear in text copied from a plain-text source, like an email message or program code.

8.4.6. Tables

Mark up tabular information using the `table` element. A table consists of one or more table rows (`tr`), each containing one or more cells of table data (`td`). Each cell can contain other block elements, such as paragraphs or lists. It can also contain another table (this nesting can repeat indefinitely). If the cell only contains one paragraph then the p element is not needed.

Example 8.8. Simple Use of `table`

Usage:

```
<p>This is a simple 2x2 table.</p>

<table>
  <tr>
    <td>Top left cell</td>

    <td>Top right cell</td>
  </tr>

  <tr>
    <td>Bottom left cell</td>

    <td>Bottom right cell</td>
  </tr>
</table>
```

A cell can span multiple rows and columns by adding the `rowspan` or `colspan` attributes with values for the number of rows or columns to be spanned.

Example 8.9. Using `rowspan`

Usage:

```
<p>One tall thin cell on the left, two short cells next to
  it on the right.</p>

<table>
```

```
  <tr>
    <td rowspan="2"> Long and thin</td>
  </tr>

  <tr>
    <td>Top cell</td>

    <td>Bottom cell</td>
  </tr>
</table>
```

Example 8.10. Using colspan

Usage:

```
<p>One long cell on top, two short cells below it.</p>

<table>
  <tr>
    <td colspan="2"> Top cell</td>
  </tr>

  <tr>
    <td>Bottom left cell</td>

    <td>Bottom right cell</td>
  </tr>
</table>
```

Example 8.11. Using rowspan and colspan Together

Usage:

```
<p>On a 3x3 grid, the top left block is a 2x2 set of
  cells merged into one.  The other cells are normal.</p>

<table>
  <tr>
    <td colspan="2" rowspan="2"> Top left large cell</td>

    <td>Top right cell</td>
  </tr>

  <tr>
    <!-- Because the large cell on the left merges into
         this row, the first <td> will occur on its
         right -->

    <td>Middle right cell</td>
  </tr>

  <tr>
    <td>Bottom left cell</td>

    <td>Bottom middle cell</td>
```

```
    <td>Bottom right cell</td>
  </tr>
</table>
```

8.5. In-line Elements

8.5.1. Emphasizing Information

Two levels of emphasis are available in XHTML, em and strong. em is for a normal level of emphasis and strong indicates stronger emphasis.

em is typically rendered in italic and strong is rendered in bold. This is not always the case, and should not be relied upon. According to best practices, web pages only hold structural and semantic information, and stylesheets are later applied to them. Think of semantics, not formatting, when using these tags.

Example 8.12. em and strong Example

Usage:

```
<p><em>This</em> has been emphasized, while
  <strong>this</strong> has been strongly emphasized.</p>
```

8.5.2. Indicating Fixed-Pitch Text

Content that should be rendered in a fixed pitch (typewriter) typeface is tagged with tt (for "teletype").

Example 8.13. tt Example

Usage:

```
<p>Many system settings are stored in
  <tt>/etc</tt>.</p>
```

8.5.3. Links

Note

Links are also inline elements.

8.5.3.1. Linking to Other Documents on the Web

A link points to the URL of a document on the web. The link is indicated with a, and the href attribute contains the URL of the target document. The content of the element becomes the link, indicated to the user by showing it in a different color or with an underline.

Example 8.14. Using `<a href="...">`

Usage:

```
<p>More information is available at the
  <a href="http://www.&os;.org/"> &os; web site</a>.</p>
```

This link always takes the user to the top of the linked document.

8.5.3.2. Linking to Specific Parts of Documents

To link to a specific point within a document, that document must include an *anchor* at the desired point. Anchors are included by setting the `id` attribute of an element to a name. This example creates an anchor by setting the `id` attribute of a p element.

Example 8.15. Creating an Anchor

Usage:

```
<p id="samplepara"> This paragraph can be referenced
  in other links with the name <tt>samplepara</tt>.</p>
```

Links to anchors are similar to plain links, but include a # symbol and the anchor's ID at the end of the URL.

Example 8.16. Linking to a Named Part of a Different Document

The `samplepara` example is part of a document called `foo.html`. A link to that specific paragraph in the document is constructed in this example.

```
<p>More information can be found in the
  <a href="foo.html#samplepara"> sample paragraph</a> of
<tt>foo.html</tt>.</p>
```

To link to a named anchor within the same document, omit the document's URL, and just use the # symbol followed by the name of the anchor.

Example 8.17. Linking to a Named Part of the Same Document

The `samplepara` example resides in this document. To link to it:

```
<p>More information can be found in the
  <a href="#samplepara"> sample paragraph</a> of this
  document.</p>
```

Chapter 9. DocBook Markup

9.1. Introduction

This chapter is an introduction to DocBook as it is used for FreeBSD documentation. DocBook is a large and complex markup system, but the subset described here covers the parts that are most widely used for FreeBSD documentation. While a moderate subset is covered, it is impossible to anticipate every situation. Please post questions that this document does not answer to the FreeBSD documentation project mailing list.

DocBook was originally developed by HaL Computer Systems and O'Reilly & Associates to be a Document Type Definition (DTD) for writing technical documentation [1]. Since 1998 it is maintained by the DocBook Technical Committee. As such, and unlike LinuxDoc and XHTML, DocBook is very heavily oriented towards markup that describes *what* something is, rather than describing *how* it should be presented.

The DocBook DTD is available from the Ports Collection in the textproc/docbook-xml port. It is automatically installed as part of the textproc/docproj port.

Formal Versus Informal

Some elements may exist in two forms, *formal* and *informal*. Typically, the formal version of the element will consist of a title followed by the informal version of the element. The informal version will not have a title.

Inline Versus Block

In the remainder of this document, when describing elements, *inline* means that the element can occur within a block element, and does not cause a line break. A *block* element, by comparison, will cause a line break (and other processing) when it is encountered.

9.2. FreeBSD Extensions

The FreeBSD Documentation Project has extended the DocBook DTD with additional elements and entities. These additions serve to make some of the markup easier or more precise.

Throughout the rest of this document, the term "DocBook" is used to mean the FreeBSD-extended DocBook DTD.

Note

Most of these extensions are not unique to FreeBSD, it was just felt that they were useful enhancements for this particular project. Should anyone from any of the other *nix camps (NetBSD, OpenBSD, Linux, …) be interested in collaborating on a standard DocBook extension set, please contact Documentation Engineering Team <doceng@FreeBSD.org>.

---

[1] A short history can be found under http://www.oasis-open.org/docbook/intro.shtml#d0e41.

9.2.1. FreeBSD Elements

The additional FreeBSD elements are not (currently) in the Ports Collection. They are stored in the FreeBSD Subversion tree, as head/share/xml/freebsd.dtd.

FreeBSD-specific elements used in the examples below are clearly marked.

9.2.2. FreeBSD Entities

This table shows some of the most useful entities available in the FDP. For a complete list, see the *.ent files in doc/share/xml .

FreeBSD Name Entities		
&os;	FreeBSD	
&os.stable;	FreeBSD-STABLE	
&os.current;	FreeBSD-CURRENT	
Manual Page Entities		
&man.ls.1;	ls(1)	Usage: &man.ls.1; is the manual page for <command>ls</command>.
&man.cp.1;	cp(1)	Usage: The manual page for <command>cp</command> is &man.cp.1;.
&man.*command*.*sectionnumber*;	*link to command manual page in section sectionnumber*	Entities are defined for all the FreeBSD manual pages.
FreeBSD Mailing List Entities		
&a.doc;	FreeBSD documentation project mailing list	Usage: A link to the &a.doc;.
&a.questions;	FreeBSD general questions mailing list	Usage: A link to the &a.questions;.
&a.*listname*;	*link to listname*	Entities are defined for all the FreeBSD mailing lists.
FreeBSD Document Link Entities		
&url.books.handbook;	https://www.FreeBSD.org/doc/en_US.ISO8859-1/books/handbook	Usage: A link to the <link xlink:href="&url.books.handbook;/advanced-networking.html">Advanced Networking</link> chapter of the Handbook.
&url.books.*bookname*;	*relative path to bookname*	Entities are defined for all the FreeBSD books.
&url.articles.committers-guide;	https://www.FreeBSD.org/doc/en_US.ISO8859-1/articles/committers-guide	Usage: A link to the <link xlink:href="&url.articles.committers-guide;">Committer's Guide</link> article.

&url.articles.*articlename*;	*relative path to* `articlename`	Entities are defined for all the Free-BSD articles.
Other Operating System Name Entities		
&linux;	Linux®	The Linux® operating system.
&unix;	UNIX®	The UNIX® operating system.
&windows;	Windows®	The Windows® operating system.
Miscellaneous Entities		
&prompt.root;	#	The root user prompt.
&prompt.user;	%	A prompt for an unprivileged user.
&postscript;	PostScript®	The PostScript® programming language.
&tex;	TeX	The TeX typesetting language.
&xorg;	Xorg	The Xorg open source X Window System.

9.3. Formal Public Identifier (FPI)

In compliance with the DocBook guidelines for writing FPIs for DocBook customizations, the FPI for the FreeBSD extended DocBook DTD is:

```
PUBLIC "-//FreeBSD//DTD DocBook V4.2-Based Extension//EN"
```

9.4. Document Structure

DocBook allows structuring documentation in several ways. The FreeBSD Documentation Project uses two primary types of DocBook document: the book and the article.

Books are organized into chapters. This is a mandatory requirement. There may be parts between the book and the chapter to provide another layer of organization. For example, the Handbook is arranged in this way.

A chapter may (or may not) contain one or more sections. These are indicated with the sect1 element. If a section contains another section then use the sect2 element, and so on, up to sect5.

Chapters and sections contain the remainder of the content.

An article is simpler than a book, and does not use chapters. Instead, the content of an article is organized into one or more sections, using the same sect1 (and sect2 and so on) elements that are used in books.

The nature of the document being written should be used to determine whether it is best marked up as a book or an article. Articles are well suited to information that does not need to be broken down into several chapters, and that is, relatively speaking, quite short, at up to 20-25 pages of content. Books are best suited to information that can be broken up into several chapters, possibly with appendices and similar content as well.

The FreeBSD tutorials are all marked up as articles, while this document, the FAQ, and the Handbook are all marked up as books, for example.

9.4.1. Starting a Book

The content of a book is contained within the book element. As well as containing structural markup, this element can contain elements that include additional information about the book. This is either meta-information, used for reference purposes, or additional content used to produce a title page.

This additional information is contained within info.

Example 9.1. Boilerplate book with info

```
<book>
  <info>
    <title>Your Title Here </title>

    <author>
      <personname>
        <firstname> Your first name </firstname>
        <surname> Your surname </surname>
      </personname>

      <affiliation>
<address>
        <email> Your email address </email>
</address>
      </affiliation>
    </author>

    <copyright>
      <year> 1998 </year>
      <holder role="mailto: your email address ">Your name </holder>
    </copyright>

    <releaseinfo> $FreeBSD$</releaseinfo>

    <abstract>
      <para>Include an abstract of the book's contents here.   </para>
    </abstract>
  </info>

  ...

</book>
```

9.4.2. Starting an Article

The content of the article is contained within the article element. As well as containing structural markup, this element can contain elements that include additional information about the article. This is either meta-information, used for reference purposes, or additional content used to produce a title page.

This additional information is contained within info.

Example 9.2. Boilerplate article with info

```
<article>
  <info>
    <title>Your title here </title>
```

```
    <author>
      <personname>
<firstname> Your first name </firstname>
<surname> Your surname </surname>
      </personname>

      <affiliation>
<address>
  <email>Your email address </email></address>
</address>
      </affiliation>
    </author>

    <copyright>
      <year>1998</year>
      <holder role="mailto: your email address ">Your name </holder>
    </copyright>

    <releaseinfo> $FreeBSD$</releaseinfo>

    <abstract>
      <para>Include an abstract of the article's contents here.   </para>
    </abstract>
  </info>

  …

</article>
```

9.4.3. Indicating Chapters

Use chapter to mark up your chapters. Each chapter has a mandatory title. Articles do not contain chapters, they are reserved for books.

Example 9.3. A Simple Chapter

```
<chapter>
  <title>The Chapter's Title</title>

  ...
</chapter>
```

A chapter cannot be empty; it must contain elements in addition to title. If you need to include an empty chapter then just use an empty paragraph.

Example 9.4. Empty Chapters

```
<chapter>
  <title>This is An Empty Chapter</title>

  <para></para>
</chapter>
```

9.4.4. Sections Below Chapters

In books, chapters may (but do not need to) be broken up into sections, subsections, and so on. In articles, sections are the main structural element, and each article must contain at least one section. Use the sect*n* element. The *n* indicates the section number, which identifies the section level.

The first sect*n* is sect1. You can have one or more of these in a chapter. They can contain one or more sect2 elements, and so on, down to sect5.

Example 9.5. Sections in Chapters

```
<chapter>
  <title>A Sample Chapter</title>

  <para>Some text in the chapter.</para>

  <sect1>
    <title>First Section</title>


    ...
  </sect1>

  <sect1>
    <title>Second Section</title>

    <sect2>
      <title>First Sub-Section</title>

      <sect3>
<title>First Sub-Sub-Section</title>

 ...
      </sect3>
    </sect2>

    <sect2>
      <title>Second Sub-Section (1.2.2)</title>

      ...
    </sect2>
  </sect1>
</chapter>
```

Note

Section numbers are automatically generated and prepended to titles when the document is rendered to an output format. The generated section numbers and titles from the example above will be:

- 1.1. First Section

- 1.2. Second Section

- 1.2.1. First Sub-Section

- 1.2.1.1. First Sub-Sub-Section

- 1.2.2. Second Sub-Section

9.4.5. Subdividing Using part Elements

parts introduce another level of organization between book and chapter with one or more parts. This cannot be done in an article.

```
<part>
  <title> Introduction</title>

  <chapter>
    <title> Overview</title>

    ...
  </chapter>

  <chapter>
    <title>What is FreeBSD?</title>

    ...
  </chapter>

  <chapter>
    <title>History</title>

    ...
  </chapter>
</part>
```

9.5. Block Elements

9.5.1. Paragraphs

DocBook supports three types of paragraphs: formalpara, para, and simpara.

Almost all paragraphs in FreeBSD documentation use para. formalpara includes a title element, and simpara disallows some elements from within para. Stick with para.

Example 9.6. para Example

Usage:

```
<para>This is a paragraph.  It can contain just about any
  other element.</para>
```

Appearance:

This is a paragraph. It can contain just about any other element.

9.5.2. Block Quotations

A block quotation is an extended quotation from another document that should not appear within the current paragraph. These are rarely needed.

Blockquotes can optionally contain a title and an attribution (or they can be left untitled and unattributed).

Example 9.7. `blockquote` Example

Usage:

```
<para>A small excerpt from the US Constitution:</para>

<blockquote>
  <title>Preamble to the Constitution of the United States</title>

  <attribution> Copied from a web site somewhere</attribution>

  <para>We the People of the United States, in Order to form a more
    perfect Union, establish Justice, insure domestic Tranquility,
    provide for the common defence, promote the general Welfare, and
    secure the Blessings of Liberty to ourselves and our Posterity, do
    ordain and establish this Constitution for the United States of
    America.</para>
</blockquote>
```

Appearance:

A small excerpt from the US Constitution:

> Preamble to the Constitution of the United States
>
> We the People of the United States, in Order to form a more perfect Union, establish Justice, insure domestic Tranquility, provide for the common defence, promote the general Welfare, and secure the Blessings of Liberty to ourselves and our Posterity, do ordain and establish this Constitution for the United States of America.
>
> —Copied from a web site somewhere

9.5.3. Tips, Notes, Warnings, Cautions, and Important Information

Extra information may need to be separated from the main body of the text. Typically this is "meta" information of which the user should be aware.

Several types of admonitions are available: tip, note, warning, caution, and important.

Which admonition to choose depends on the situation. The DocBook documentation suggests:

- Note is for information that should be heeded by all readers.

- Important is a variation on Note.

- Caution is for information regarding possible data loss or software damage.

- Warning is for information regarding possible hardware damage or injury to life or limb.

Example 9.8. `tip` and `important` Example

Usage:

```
<tip>
  <para>&os; may reduce stress.</para>
</tip>
```

```
<important>
  <para>Please use admonitions sparingly.  Too many admonitions
    are visually jarring and can have the opposite of the
    intended effect.</para>
</important>
```

Appearance:

Tip

FreeBSD may reduce stress.

Important

Please use admonitions sparingly. Too many admonitions are visually jarring and can have the opposite of the intended effect.

9.5.4. Examples

Examples can be shown with `example`.

Example 9.9. `example` Source

Usage:

```
<example>
  <para>Empty files can be created easily:</para>

  <screen>&prompt.user; <userinput> touch file1 file2 file3</userinput> </screen>
</example>
```

Appearance:

Example 9.10. Rendered `example`

Empty files can be created easily:

```
% touch file1 file2 file3
```

9.5.5. Lists and Procedures

Information often needs to be presented as lists, or as a number of steps that must be carried out in order to accomplish a particular goal.

To do this, use `itemizedlist`, `orderedlist`, `variablelist`, or `procedure`. There are other types of list elements in DocBook, but we will not cover them here.

`itemizedlist` and `orderedlist` are similar to their counterparts in HTML, `ul` and `ol`. Each one consists of one or more `listitem` elements, and each `listitem` contains one or more block elements. The `listitem` elements are analogous to HTML's `li` tags. However, unlike HTML, they are required.

Example 9.11. `itemizedlist` and `orderedlist` Example

Usage:

```
<itemizedlist>
  <listitem>
    <para>This is the first itemized item.</para>
  </listitem>

  <listitem>
    <para>This is the second itemized item.</para>
  </listitem>
</itemizedlist>

<orderedlist>
  <listitem>
    <para>This is the first ordered item.</para>
  </listitem>

  <listitem>
    <para>This is the second ordered item.</para>
  </listitem>
</orderedlist>
```

Appearance:

- This is the first itemized item.

- This is the second itemized item.

1. This is the first ordered item.

2. This is the second ordered item.

An alternate and often useful way of presenting information is the `variablelist`. These are lists where each entry has a term and a description. They are well suited for many types of descriptions, and present information in a form that is often easier for the reader than sections and subsections.

A `variablelist` has a `title`, and then pairs of `term` and `listitem` entries.

Example 9.12. `variablelist` Example

Usage:

```
<variablelist>
  <varlistentry>
    <term>Parallel</term>
```

```
      <listitem>
        <para>In parallel communications, groups of bits arrive
  at the same time over multiple communications
  channels.</para>
      </listitem>
    </varlistentry>

    <varlistentry>
      <term>Serial</term>

      <listitem>
        <para>In serial communications, bits arrive one at a
  time over a single communications
  channel.</para>
      </listitem>
    </varlistentry>
  </variablelist>
```

Appearance:

Parallel
    In parallel communications, groups of bits arrive at the same time over multiple communications
    channels.

Serial
    In serial communications, bits arrive one at a time over a single communications channel.

A procedure shows a series of steps, which may in turn consist of more steps or substeps. Each step contains block elements and may include an optional title.

Sometimes, steps are not sequential, but present a choice: do *this* or do *that*, but not both. For these alternative choices, use stepalternatives.

Example 9.13. procedure Example

Usage:

```
<procedure>
  <step>
    <para>Do this.</para>
  </step>

  <step>
    <para>Then do this.</para>
  </step>

  <step>
    <para>And now do this.</para>
  </step>

  <step>
    <para>Finally, do one of these.</para>

    <stepalternatives>
      <step>
<para>Go left.</para>
      </step>

      <step>
```

```
    <para>Go right.</para>
        </step>
      </stepalternatives>
    </step>
</procedure>
```

Appearance:

1. Do this.

2. Then do this.

3. And now do this.

4. Finally, do one of these:

    •   Go left.

    •   Go right.

9.5.6. Showing File Samples

Fragments of a file (or perhaps a complete file) are shown by wrapping them in the `programlisting` element.

White space and line breaks within `programlisting` *are* significant. In particular, this means that the opening tag should appear on the same line as the first line of the output, and the closing tag should appear on the same line as the last line of the output, otherwise spurious blank lines may be included.

Example 9.14. `programlisting` Example

Usage:

```
<para>When finished, the program will look like
  this:</para>

<programlisting> #include &lt;stdio.h&gt;

int
main(void)
{
    printf("hello, world\n");
    return 0;
}</programlisting>
```

Notice how the angle brackets in the `#include` line need to be referenced by their entities instead of being included literally.

Appearance:

When finished, the program will look like this:

```
#include <stdio.h>

int
main(void)
{
    printf("hello, world\n");
    return 0;
```

```
}
```

9.5.7. Callouts

A callout is a visual marker for referring to a piece of text or specific position within an example.

Callouts are marked with the co element. Each element must have a unique id assigned to it. After the example, include a calloutlist that describes each callout.

Example 9.15. `co` and `calloutlist` Example

```
<para>When finished, the program will look like
  this:</para>

<programlisting> #include &lt;stdio.h&gt; <co xml:id="co-ex-include"/>

int <co xml:id="co-ex-return"/>
main(void)
{
    printf("hello, world\n"); <co xml:id="co-ex-printf"/>
}</programlisting>

<calloutlist>
  <callout arearefs="co-ex-include">
    <para>Includes the standard IO header file.</para>
  </callout>

  <callout arearefs="co-ex-return">
    <para>Specifies that <function>main()</function> returns an
      int.</para>
  </callout>

  <callout arearefs="co-ex-printf">
    <para>The <function>printf()</function> call that writes
      <literal>hello, world</literal> to standard output.</para>
  </callout>
</calloutlist>
```

Appearance:

When finished, the program will look like this:

```
#include <stdio.h> ❶

int ❷
main(void)
{
    printf("hello, world\n"); ❸
}
```

❶   Includes the standard IO header file.
❷   Specifies that main() returns an int.
❸   The printf() call that writes hello, world to standard output.

9.5.8. Tables

Unlike HTML, DocBook does not need tables for layout purposes, as the stylesheet handles those issues. Instead, just use tables for marking up tabular data.

In general terms (and see the DocBook documentation for more detail) a table (which can be either formal or informal) consists of a `table` element. This contains at least one `tgroup` element, which specifies (as an attribute) the number of columns in this table group. Within the tablegroup there is one `thead` element, which contains elements for the table headings (column headings), and one `tbody` which contains the body of the table.

Both `tgroup` and `thead` contain row elements, which in turn contain `entry` elements. Each `entry` element specifies one cell in the table.

Example 9.16. `informaltable` Example

Usage:

```
<informaltable pgwide="1">
  <tgroup cols="2">
    <thead>
      <row>
        <entry>This is Column Head 1</entry>
        <entry>This is Column Head 2</entry>
      </row>
    </thead>

    <tbody>
      <row>
<entry>Row 1, column 1</entry>
<entry>Row 1, column 2</entry>
      </row>

      <row>
<entry>Row 2, column 1</entry>
<entry>Row 2, column 2</entry>
      </row>
    </tbody>
  </tgroup>
</informaltable>
```

Appearance:

This is Column Head 1	This is Column Head 2
Row 1, column 1	Row 1, column 2
Row 2, column 1	Row 2, column 2

Always use the `pgwide` attribute with a value of 1 with the `informaltable` element. A bug in Internet Explorer can cause the table to render incorrectly if this is omitted.

Table borders can be suppressed by setting the `frame` attribute to none in the `informaltable` element. For example, `informaltable frame="none"` .

Example 9.17. Table with `frame="none"` Example

Appearance:

This is Column Head 1	This is Column Head 2
Row 1, column 1	Row 1, column 2

This is Column Head 1	This is Column Head 2
Row 2, column 1	Row 2, column 2

9.5.9. Examples for the User to Follow

Examples for the user to follow are often necessary. Typically, these will consist of dialogs with the computer; the user types in a command, the user gets a response back, the user types another command, and so on.

A number of distinct elements and entities come into play here.

screen
> Everything the user sees in this example will be on the computer screen, so the next element is screen.

> Within screen, white space is significant.

prompt, &prompt.root; and &prompt.user;
> Some of the things the user will be seeing on the screen are prompts from the computer (either from the operating system, command shell, or application). These should be marked up using prompt.

> As a special case, the two shell prompts for the normal user and the root user have been provided as entities. To indicate the user is at a shell prompt, use one of &prompt.root; and &prompt.user; as necessary. They do not need to be inside prompt.

> ### Note
>
> &prompt.root; and &prompt.user; are FreeBSD extensions to DocBook, and are not part of the original DTD.

userinput
> When displaying text that the user should type in, wrap it in userinput tags. It will be displayed differently than system output text.

Example 9.18. `screen`, `prompt`, and `userinput` Example

Usage:

```
<screen>&prompt.user; <userinput> ls -1</userinput>
foo1
foo2
foo3
&prompt.user; <userinput> ls -1 | grep foo2</userinput>
foo2
&prompt.user; <userinput> su</userinput>
<prompt> Password: </prompt>
&prompt.root; <userinput> cat foo2</userinput>
This is the file called 'foo2'</screen>
```

Appearance:

```
% ls -1
foo1
foo2
```

```
foo3
% ls -l | grep foo2
foo2
% su
Password:
# cat foo2
This is the file called 'foo2'
```

 Note

Even though we are displaying the contents of the file foo2, it is *not* marked up as program-listing. Reserve programlisting for showing fragments of files outside the context of user actions.

9.6. In-line Elements

9.6.1. Emphasizing Information

To emphasize a particular word or phrase, use emphasis. This may be presented as italic, or bold, or might be spoken differently with a text-to-speech system.

There is no way to change the presentation of the emphasis within the document, no equivalent of HTML's b and i. If the information being presented is important, then consider presenting it in important rather than emphasis.

Example 9.19. emphasis Example

Usage:

```
<para>&os; is without doubt <emphasis> the</emphasis>
  premiere &unix;-like operating system for the Intel
  architecture.</para>
```

Appearance:

FreeBSD is without doubt *the* premiere UNIX®-like operating system for the Intel architecture.

9.6.2. Acronyms

Many computer terms are *acronyms*, words formed from the first letter of each word in a phrase. Acronyms are marked up into acronym elements. It is helpful to the reader when an acronym is defined on the first use, as shown in the example below.

Example 9.20. acronym Example

Usage:

```
<para>Request For Comments (<acronym>RFC</acronym> ) 1149
  defined the use of avian carriers for transmission of
```

```
Internet Protocol (<acronym> IP</acronym> ) data.    The
quantity of <acronym> IP</acronym>  data currently
transmitted in that manner is unknown.</para>
```

Appearance:

Request For Comments (RFC) 1149 defined the use of avian carriers for transmission of Internet Protocol (IP) data. The quantity of IP data currently transmitted in that manner is unknown.

9.6.3. Quotations

To quote text from another document or source, or to denote a phrase that is used figuratively, use quote. Most of the markup tags available for normal text are also available from within a quote.

Example 9.21. quote Example

Usage:

```
<para>However, make sure that the search does not go beyond the
  <quote>boundary between local and public administration</quote> ,
  as <acronym> RFC</acronym>  1535 calls it.</para>
```

Appearance:

However, make sure that the search does not go beyond the "boundary between local and public administration", as RFC 1535 calls it.

9.6.4. Keys, Mouse Buttons, and Combinations

To refer to a specific key on the keyboard, use keycap. To refer to a mouse button, use mousebutton. And to refer to combinations of key presses or mouse clicks, wrap them all in keycombo.

keycombo has an attribute called action, which may be one of click, double-click, other, press, seq, or simul. The last two values denote whether the keys or buttons should be pressed in sequence, or simultaneously.

The stylesheets automatically add any connecting symbols, such as +, between the key names, when wrapped in keycombo.

Example 9.22. Keys, Mouse Buttons, and Combinations Example

Usage:

```
<para>To switch to the second virtual terminal, press
  <keycombo action="simul"> <keycap> Alt</keycap>
    <keycap> F1</keycap> </keycombo> .</para>

<para>To exit <command> vi</command>  without saving changes, type
  <keycombo action="seq"> <keycap> Esc</keycap> <keycap> :</keycap>
    <keycap> q</keycap> <keycap> !</keycap> </keycombo> .</para>

<para>My window manager is configured so that
  <keycombo action="simul"> <keycap> Alt</keycap>
    <mousebutton> right</mousebutton>
  </keycombo>  mouse button is used to move windows.</para>
```

Appearance:

To switch to the second virtual terminal, press Alt+F1.

To exit vi without saving changes, type Esc : q !.

My window manager is configured so that Alt+right mouse button is used to move windows.

9.6.5. Applications, Commands, Options, and Cites

Both applications and commands are frequently referred to when writing documentation. The distinction between them is that an application is the name of a program or suite of programs that fulfill a particular task. A command is the filename of a program that the user can type and run at a command line.

It is often necessary to show some of the options that a command might take.

Finally, it is often useful to list a command with its manual section number, in the "command(number)" format so common in Unix manuals.

Mark up application names with application.

To list a command with its manual section number (which should be most of the time) the DocBook element is citerefentry. This will contain a further two elements, refentrytitle and manvolnum. The content of refentrytitle is the name of the command, and the content of manvolnum is the manual page section.

This can be cumbersome to write, and so a series of general entities have been created to make this easier. Each entity takes the form &man.*manual-page*.*manual-section*;.

The file that contains these entities is in doc/share/xml/man-refs.ent , and can be referred to using this FPI:

```
PUBLIC "-//FreeBSD//ENTITIES DocBook Manual Page Entities//EN"
```

Therefore, the introduction to FreeBSD documentation will usually include this:

```
<!DOCTYPE book PUBLIC "-//FreeBSD//DTD DocBook V4.1-Based Extension//EN" [

<!ENTITY % man PUBLIC "-//FreeBSD//ENTITIES DocBook Manual Page Entities//EN">
%man;

...

]>
```

Use command to include a command name "in-line" but present it as something the user should type.

Use option to mark up the options which will be passed to a command.

When referring to the same command multiple times in close proximity, it is preferred to use the &man.*command*.*section*; notation to markup the first reference and use command to markup subsequent references. This makes the generated output, especially HTML, appear visually better.

Example 9.23. Applications, Commands, and Options Example

Usage:

```
<para><application> Sendmail</application>  is the most
  widely used Unix mail application.<para>
```

```
<para><application> Sendmail</application>  includes the
  <citerefentry>
    <refentrytitle> sendmail</refentrytitle>
    <manvolnum> 8</manvolnum>
  </citerefentry> , &man.mailq.1;, and &man.newaliases.1;
  programs.</para>

<para>One of the command line parameters to <citerefentry>
    <refentrytitle> sendmail</refentrytitle>
    <manvolnum> 8</manvolnum>
  </citerefentry> , <option> -bp</option> , will display the current
  status of messages in the mail queue.  Check this on the command
  line by running <command> sendmail -bp</command> .</para>
```

Appearance:

Sendmail is the most widely used Unix mail application.

Sendmail includes the sendmail(8), mailq(1), and newaliases(1) programs.

One of the command line parameters to sendmail(8), -bp, will display the current status of messages in the mail queue. Check this on the command line by running sendmail -bp.

Note

Notice how the &man. *command.section*; notation is easier to follow.

9.6.6. Files, Directories, Extensions, Device Names

To refer to the name of a file, a directory, a file extension, or a device name, use filename.

Example 9.24. filename Example

Usage:

```
<para>The source for the Handbook in English is found in
  <filename> /usr/doc/en_US.ISO8859-1/books/handbook/</filename> .
  The main file is called <filename> book.xml</filename> .
  There is also a <filename>Makefile</filename>  and a
  number of files with a <filename> .ent</filename>  extension.</para>

<para><filename> kbd0</filename>  is the first keyboard detected
  by the system, and appears in
  <filename> /dev</filename> .</para>
```

Appearance:

The source for the Handbook in English is found in /usr/doc/en_US.ISO8859-1/books/handbook/ . The main file is called book.xml . There is also a Makefile and a number of files with a .ent extension.

kbd0 is the first keyboard detected by the system, and appears in /dev.

9.6.7. The Name of Ports

FreeBSD Extension

These elements are part of the FreeBSD extension to DocBook, and do not exist in the original DocBook DTD.

To include the name of a program from the FreeBSD Ports Collection in the document, use the `package` tag. Since the Ports Collection can be installed in any number of locations, only include the category and the port name; do not include `/usr/ports` .

By default, `package` refers to a binary package. To refer to a port that will be built from source, set the `role` attribute to `port`.

Example 9.25. `package` Example

Usage:

```
<para>Install the <package>net/wireshark</package> binary
  package to view network traffic.</para>

<para><package role="port">net/wireshark</package> can also be
  built and installed from the Ports Collection.</para>
```

Appearance:

Install the net/wireshark binary package to view network traffic.

net/wireshark can also be built and installed from the Ports Collection.

9.6.8. Hosts, Domains, IP Addresses, User Names, Group Names, and Other System Items

FreeBSD Extension

These elements are part of the FreeBSD extension to DocBook, and do not exist in the original DocBook DTD.

Information for "system items" is marked up with `systemitem`. The `class` attribute is used to identify the particular type of information shown.

`class="domainname"`
   The text is a domain name, such as `FreeBSD.org` or `ngo.org.uk` . There is no hostname component.

`class="etheraddress"`
   The text is an Ethernet MAC address, expressed as a series of 2 digit hexadecimal numbers separated by colons.

`class="fqdomainname"`
   The text is a Fully Qualified Domain Name, with both hostname and domain name parts.

`class="ipaddress"`
   The text is an IP address, probably expressed as a dotted quad.

class="netmask"
> The text is a network mask, which might be expressed as a dotted quad, a hexadecimal string, or as a / followed by a number (CIDR notation).

class="systemname"
> With class="systemname" the marked up information is the simple hostname, such as freefall or wcarchive.

class="username"
> The text is a username, like root.

class="groupname"
> The text is a groupname, like wheel.

Example 9.26. systemitem and Classes Example

Usage:

```
<para>The local machine can always be referred to by the
  name <systemitem class="systemname"> localhost</systemitem> , which will have the ↵
IP
  address <systemitem class="ipaddress"> 127.0.0.1</systemitem> .</para>

<para>The <systemitem class="domainname"> FreeBSD.org</systemitem>
  domain contains a number of different hosts, including
  <systemitem class="fqdomainname"> freefall.FreeBSD.org</systemitem> and
  <systemitem class="fqdomainname"> bento.FreeBSD.org</systemitem> .</para>

<para>When adding an <acronym> IP</acronym> alias to an
  interface (using <command> ifconfig</command> )
  <emphasis> always</emphasis> use a netmask of
  <systemitem class="netmask"> 255.255.255.255</systemitem> (which can
  also be expressed as
  <systemitem class="netmask"> 0xffffffff</systemitem> ).</para>

<para>The <acronym> MAC</acronym> address uniquely identifies
  every network card in existence.  A typical
  <acronym> MAC</acronym> address looks like
  <systemitem class="etheraddress"> 08:00:20:87:ef:d0</systemitem> .</para>

<para>To carry out most system administration functions
  requires logging in as <systemitem class="username"> root</systemitem> .</para>
```

Appearance:

The local machine can always be referred to by the name localhost, which will have the IP address 127.0.0.1.

The FreeBSD.org domain contains a number of different hosts, including freefall.FreeBSD.org and bento.FreeBSD.org.

When adding an IP alias to an interface (using ifconfig) *always* use a netmask of 255.255.255.255 (which can also be expressed as 0xffffffff).

The MAC address uniquely identifies every network card in existence. A typical MAC address looks like 08:00:20:87:ef:d0 .

To carry out most system administration functions requires logging in as root.

9.6.9. Uniform Resource Identifiers (URIs)

Occasionally it is useful to show a Uniform Resource Identifier (URI) without making it an active hyperlink. The `uri` element makes this possible:

Example 9.27. `uri` Example

Usage:

```
<para>This URL shows only as text:
  <uri>https://www.FreeBSD.org</uri>.  It does not
  create a link.</para>
```

Appearance:

This URL shows only as text: https://www.FreeBSD.org . It does not create a link.

To create links, see Section 9.8, "Links".

9.6.10. Email Addresses

Email addresses are marked up as `email` elements. In the HTML output format, the wrapped text becomes a hyperlink to the email address. Other output formats that support hyperlinks may also make the email address into a link.

Example 9.28. `email` with a Hyperlink Example

Usage:

```
<para>An email address that does not actually exist, like
  <email>notreal@example.com</email>, can be used as an
  example.</para>
```

Appearance:

An email address that does not actually exist, like <notreal@example.com>, can be used as an example.

A FreeBSD-specific extension allows setting the `role` attribute to `nolink` to prevent the creation of the hyperlink to the email address.

Example 9.29. `email` Without a Hyperlink Example

Usage:

```
<para>Sometimes a link to an email address like
  <email role="nolink"> notreal@example.com</email> is not
  desired.</para>
```

Appearance:

Sometimes a link to an email address like <notreal@example.com> is not desired.

9.6.11. Describing Makefiles

 FreeBSD Extension

These elements are part of the FreeBSD extension to DocBook, and do not exist in the original DocBook DTD.

Two elements exist to describe parts of Makefiles, buildtarget and varname.

buildtarget identifies a build target exported by a Makefile that can be given as a parameter to make. varname identifies a variable that can be set (in the environment, on the command line with make, or within the Makefile) to influence the process.

Example 9.30. buildtarget and varname Example

Usage:

```
<para>Two common targets in a <filename> Makefile</filename>
  are <buildtarget> all</buildtarget>  and
  <buildtarget> clean</buildtarget> .</para>

<para>Typically, invoking <buildtarget> all</buildtarget>  will
  rebuild the application, and invoking
  <buildtarget> clean</buildtarget>  will remove the temporary
  files (<filename> .o</filename>  for example) created by the
  build process.</para>

<para><buildtarget> clean</buildtarget>  may be controlled by a
  number of variables, including <varname> CLOBBER</varname>
  and <varname> RECURSE</varname> .</para>
```

Appearance:

Two common targets in a Makefile are all and clean.

Typically, invoking all will rebuild the application, and invoking clean will remove the temporary files (.o for example) created by the build process.

clean may be controlled by a number of variables, including CLOBBER and RECURSE.

9.6.12. Literal Text

Literal text, or text which should be entered verbatim, is often needed in documentation. This is text that is excerpted from another file, or which should be copied exactly as shown from the documentation into another file.

Some of the time, programlisting will be sufficient to denote this text. But programlisting is not always appropriate, particularly when you want to include a portion of a file "in-line" with the rest of the paragraph.

On these occasions, use literal.

Example 9.31. literal Example

Usage:

```
<para>The <literal> maxusers 10</literal>  line in the kernel
    configuration file determines the size of many system tables, and is
    a rough guide to how many simultaneous logins the system will
    support.</para>
```

Appearance:

The maxusers 10 line in the kernel configuration file determines the size of many system tables, and is a rough guide to how many simultaneous logins the system will support.

9.6.13. Showing Items That the User Must Fill In

There will often be times when the user is shown what to do, or referred to a file or command line, but cannot simply copy the example provided. Instead, they must supply some information themselves.

replaceable is designed for this eventuality. Use it *inside* other elements to indicate parts of that element's content that the user must replace.

Example 9.32. replaceable Example

Usage:

```
<screen> &prompt.user; <userinput> man <replaceable> command</replaceable> </
userinput> </screen>
```

Appearance:

```
% man command
```

replaceable can be used in many different elements, including literal. This example also shows that replaceable should only be wrapped around the content that the user *is* meant to provide. The other content should be left alone.

Usage:

```
<para>The <literal> maxusers <replaceable> n</replaceable> </literal>
    line in the kernel configuration file determines the size of many system
    tables, and is a rough guide to how many simultaneous logins the system will
    support.</para>

<para>For a desktop workstation, <literal> 32</literal>  is a good value
    for <replaceable> n</replaceable> .</para>
```

Appearance:

The maxusers *n* line in the kernel configuration file determines the size of many system tables, and is a rough guide to how many simultaneous logins the system will support.

For a desktop workstation, 32 is a good value for *n*.

9.6.14. Showing GUI Buttons

Buttons presented by a graphical user interface are marked with guibutton. To make the text look more like a graphical button, brackets and non-breaking spaces are added surrounding the text.

Example 9.33. guibutton Example

Usage:

```
<para>Edit the file, then click
  <guibutton> [ Save ]</guibutton>  to save the
  changes.</para>
```

Appearance:

Edit the file, then click [Save] to save the changes.

9.6.15. Quoting System Errors

System errors generated by FreeBSD are marked with errorname. This indicates the exact error that appears.

Example 9.34. errorname Example

Usage:

```
<screen> <errorname> Panic: cannot mount root</errorname> </screen>
```

Appearance:

```
Panic: cannot mount root
```

9.7. Images

 Important

Image support in the documentation is somewhat experimental. The mechanisms described here are unlikely to change, but that is not guaranteed.

To provide conversion between different image formats, the graphics/ImageMagick port must be installed. This port is not included in the textproc/docproj meta port, and must be installed separately.

A good example of the use of images is the doc/en_US.ISO8859-1/articles/vm-design/ document. Examine the files in that directory to see how these elements are used together. Build different output formats to see how the format determines what images are shown in the rendered document.

9.7.1. Image Formats

The following image formats are currently supported. An image file will automatically be converted to bitmap or vector image depending on the output document format.

These are the *only* formats in which images should be committed to the documentation repository.

EPS (Encapsulated Postscript)
: Images that are primarily vector based, such as network diagrams, time lines, and similar, should be in this format. These images have a `.eps` extension.

PNG (Portable Network Graphic)
: For bitmaps, such as screen captures, use this format. These images have the `.png` extension.

PIC (PIC graphics language)
: PIC is a language for drawing simple vector-based figures used in the pic(1) utility. These images have the `.pic` extension.

SCR (SCReen capture)
: This format is specific to screenshots of console output. The following command generates an SCR file `shot.scr` from video buffer of `/dev/ttyv0` :

```
# vidcontrol -p < /dev/ttyv0 > shot.scr
```

This is preferable to PNG format for screenshots because the SCR file contains plain text of the command lines so that it can be converted to a PNG image or a plain text depending on the output document format.

Use the appropriate format for each image. Documentation will often have a mix of EPS and PNG images. The `Makefiles` ensure that the correct format image is chosen depending on the output format used. *Do not commit the same image to the repository in two different formats.*

Important

The Documentation Project may eventually switch to using the SVG (Scalable Vector Graphic) format for vector images. However, the current state of SVG capable editing tools makes this impractical.

9.7.2. Image File Locations

Image files can be stored in one of several locations, depending on the document and image:

- In the same directory as the document itself, usually done for articles and small books that keep all their files in a single directory.

- In a subdirectory of the main document. Typically done when a large book uses separate subdirectories to organize individual chapters.

  When images are stored in a subdirectory of the main document directory, the subdirectory name must be included in their paths in the `Makefile` and the `imagedata` element.

- In a subdirectory of `doc/share/images` named after the document. For example, images for the Handbook are stored in `doc/share/images/books/handbook` . Images that work for multiple translations are stored in this upper level of the documentation file tree. Generally, these are images that can be used unchanged in non-English translations of the document.

9.7.3. Image Markup

Images are included as part of a `mediaobject`. The `mediaobject` can contain other, more specific objects. We are concerned with two, the `imageobject` and the `textobject`.

Include one `imageobject`, and two `textobject` elements. The `imageobject` will point to the name of the image file without the extension. The `textobject` elements contain information that will be presented to the user as well as, or instead of, the image itself.

Text elements are shown to the reader in several situations. When the document is viewed in HTML, text elements are shown while the image is loading, or if the mouse pointer is hovered over the image, or if a text-only browser is being used. In formats like plain text where graphics are not possible, the text elements are shown instead of the graphical ones.

This example shows how to include an image called `fig1.png` in a document. The image is a rectangle with an A inside it:

```
<mediaobject>
  <imageobject>
    <imagedata fileref="fig1"/>  ❶
  </imageobject>

  <textobject>
    <literallayout class="monospaced">  +---------------+ ❷
|        A        |
+---------------+</literallayout>
  </textobject>

  <textobject>
    <phrase>A picture</phrase>  ❸
  </textobject>
</mediaobject>
```

❶ Include an `imagedata` element inside the `imageobject` element. The `fileref` attribute should contain the filename of the image to include, without the extension. The stylesheets will work out which extension should be added to the filename automatically.

❷ The first `textobject` contains a `literallayout` element, where the `class` attribute is set to `monospaced`. This is an opportunity to demonstrate ASCII art skills. This content will be used if the document is converted to plain text.

Notice how the first and last lines of the content of the `literallayout` element butt up next to the element's tags. This ensures no extraneous white space is included.

❸ The second `textobject` contains a single `phrase` element. The contents of this phrase will become the `alt` attribute for the image when this document is converted to HTML.

9.7.4. Image Makefile Entries

Images must be listed in the `Makefile` in the `IMAGES` variable. This variable must contain the names of all the *source* images. For example, if there are three figures, `fig1.eps` , `fig2.png`, `fig3.png`, then the `Makefile` should have lines like this in it.

```
...
IMAGES= fig1.eps fig2.png fig3.png
...
```

or

```
...
IMAGES=  fig1.eps
IMAGES+= fig2.png
IMAGES+= fig3.png
...
```

Again, the `Makefile` will work out the complete list of images it needs to build the source document, you only need to list the image files *you* provided.

9.7.5. Images and Chapters in Subdirectories

Be careful when separating documentation into smaller files in different directories (see Section 7.7.1, "Using General Entities to Include Files").

Suppose there is a book with three chapters, and the chapters are stored in their own directories, called chapter1/chapter.xml, chapter2/chapter.xml, and chapter3/chapter.xml. If each chapter has images associated with it, place those images in each chapter's subdirectory (chapter1/, chapter2/, and chapter3/).

However, doing this requires including the directory names in the IMAGES variable in the Makefile, *and* including the directory name in the imagedata element in the document.

For example, if the book has chapter1/fig1.png, then chapter1/chapter.xml should contain:

```
<mediaobject>
  <imageobject>
    <imagedata fileref="chapter1/fig1"/>     ❶
  </imageobject>

  ...

</mediaobject>
```

❶   The directory name must be included in the fileref attribute.

The Makefile must contain:

```
...
IMAGES=  chapter1/fig1.png
...
```

9.8. Links

Note

Links are also in-line elements. To show a URI without creating a link, see Section 9.6.9, "Uniform Resource Identifiers (URIs)".

9.8.1. xml:id Attributes

Most DocBook elements accept an xml:id attribute to give that part of the document a unique name. The xml:id can be used as a target for a crossreference or link.

Any portion of the document that will be a link target must have an xml:id attribute. Assigning an xml:id to all chapters and sections, even if there are no current plans to link to them, is a good idea. These xml:ids can be used as unique reference points by anyone referring to the HTML version of the document.

Example 9.35. xml:id on Chapters and Sections Example

```
<chapter xml:id="introduction">
  <title>Introduction</title>

  <para>This is the introduction.  It contains a subsection,
    which is identified as well.</para>

  <sect1 xml:id="introduction-moredetails">
    <title>More Details</title>

    <para>This is a subsection.</para>
  </sect1>
```

```
</chapter>
```

Use descriptive values for `xml:id` names. The values must be unique within the entire document, not just in a single file. In the example, the subsection `xml:id` is constructed by appending text to the chapter `xml:id`. This ensures that the `xml:id`s are unique. It also helps both reader and anyone editing the document to see where the link is located within the document, similar to a directory path to a file.

9.8.2. Crossreferences with `xref`

`xref` provides the reader with a link to jump to another section of the document. The target `xml:id` is specified in the `linkend` attribute, and `xref` generates the link text automatically.

Example 9.36. `xref` Example

Assume that this fragment appears somewhere in a document that includes the `xml:id` example shown above:

```
<para>More information can be found
  in <xref linkend="introduction"/>  .</para>

<para>More specific information can be found
  in <xref linkend="introduction-moredetails"/>   .</para>
```

The link text will be generated automatically, looking like (*emphasized* text indicates the link text):

> More information can be found in *Chapter 1, Introduction*.
>
> More specific information can be found in *Section 1.1, "More Details"*.

The link text is generated automatically from the chapter and section number and `title` elements.

9.8.3. Linking to Other Documents on the Web

The link element described here allows the writer to define the link text. When link text is used, it is very important to be descriptive to give the reader an idea of where the link goes. Remember that DocBook can be rendered to multiple types of media. The reader might be looking at a printed book or other form of media where there are no links. If the link text is not descriptive enough, the reader might not be able to locate the linked section.

The `xlink:href` attribute is the URL of the page, and the content of the element is the text that will be displayed for the user to activate.

In many situations, it is preferable to show the actual URL rather than text. This can be done by leaving out the element text entirely.

Example 9.37. `link` to a FreeBSD Documentation Web Page Example

Link to the book or article URL entity. To link to a specific chapter in a book, add a slash and the chapter file name, followed by an optional anchor within the chapter. For articles, link to the article URL entity, followed by an optional anchor within the article. URL entities can be found in `doc/share/xml/urls.ent` .

Usage for FreeBSD book links:

```
<para>Read the <link
    xlink:href="&url.books.handbook;/svn.html#svn-intro">  SVN
    introduction</link>, then pick the nearest mirror from
  the list of <link
    xlink:href="&url.books.handbook;/svn.html#svn-mirrors">  Subversion
    mirror sites</link> .</para>
```

Appearance:

Read the SVN introduction, then pick the nearest mirror from the list of Subversion mirror sites.

Usage for FreeBSD article links:

```
<para>Read this
  <link xlink:href="&url.articles.bsdl-gpl;">  article
    about the BSD license</link>, or just the
  <link xlink:href="&url.articles.bsdl-gpl;#intro">   introduction</link> .</para>
```

Appearance:

Read this article about the BSD license, or just the introduction.

Example 9.38. link to a FreeBSD Web Page Example

Usage:

```
<para>Of course, you could stop reading this document and go to the
  <link xlink:href="&url.base;/index.html">  FreeBSD home page</link>  instead.</para>
```

Appearance:

Of course, you could stop reading this document and go to the FreeBSD home page instead.

Example 9.39. link to an External Web Page Example

Usage:

```
<para>Wikipedia has an excellent reference on
  <link
    xlink:href="http://en.wikipedia.org/wiki/GUID_Partition_Table">   GUID
    Partition Tables</link> .</para>
```

Appearance:

Wikipedia has an excellent reference on GUID Partition Tables.

The link text can be omitted to show the actual URL:

```
<para>Wikipedia has an excellent reference on
  GUID Partition Tables: <link
    xlink:href="http://en.wikipedia.org/wiki/GUID_Partition_Table">   </link> .</para>
```

The same link can be entered using shorter notation instead of a separate ending tag:

```
<para>Wikipedia has an excellent reference on
  GUID Partition Tables: <link
```

```
    xlink:href="http://en.wikipedia.org/wiki/GUID_Partition_Table"/>    .</para>
```

The two methods are equivalent. Appearance:

Wikipedia has an excellent reference on GUID Partition Tables: `http://en.wikipedia.org/wiki/GUID_Partition_Table`.

Chapter 10. Style Sheets

XML is concerned with content, and says nothing about how that content should be presented to the reader or rendered on paper. Multiple *style sheet* languages have been developed to describe visual layout, including Extensible Stylesheet Language Transformation (XSLT), Document Style Semantics and Specification Language (DSSSL), and Cascading Style Sheets (CSS).

The FDP documents use XSLT stylesheets to transform DocBook into XHTML, and then CSS formatting is applied to the XHTML pages. Printable output is currently rendered with legacy DSSSL stylesheets, but this will probably change in the future.

10.1. CSS

Cascading Style Sheets (CSS) are a mechanism for attaching style information (font, weight, size, color, and so forth) to elements in an XHTML document without abusing XHTML to do so.

10.1.1. The DocBook Documents

The FreeBSD XSLT and DSSSL stylesheets refer to `docbook.css`, which is expected to be present in the same directory as the XHTML files. The project-wide CSS file is copied from `doc/share/misc/docbook.css` when documents are converted to XHTML, and is installed automatically.

Chapter 11. Translations

This is the FAQ for people translating the FreeBSD documentation (FAQ, Handbook, tutorials, manual pages, and others) to different languages.

It is *very* heavily based on the translation FAQ from the FreeBSD German Documentation Project, originally written by Frank Gründer <elwood@mc5sys.in-berlin.de> and translated back to English by Bernd Warken <bwarken@mayn.de >.

The FAQ is maintained by the Documentation Engineering Team <doceng@FreeBSD.org>.

Q: What do i18n and l10n mean?

A: i18n means internationalization and l10n means localization. They are just a convenient shorthand.

      i18n can be read as "i" followed by 18 letters, followed by "n". Similarly, l10n is "l" followed by 10 letters, followed by "n".

Q: Is there a mailing list for translators?

A: Yes. Different translation groups have their own mailing lists. The list of translation projects has more information about the mailing lists and web sites run by each translation project. In addition there is <freebsd-translators@freebsd.org> for general translation discussion.

Q: Are more translators needed?

A: Yes. The more people work on translation the faster it gets done, and the faster changes to the English documentation are mirrored in the translated documents.

      You do not have to be a professional translator to be able to help.

Q: What languages do I need to know?

A: Ideally, you will have a good knowledge of written English, and obviously you will need to be fluent in the language you are translating to.

      English is not strictly necessary. For example, you could do a Hungarian translation of the FAQ from the Spanish translation.

Q: What software do I need to know?

A: It is strongly recommended that you maintain a local copy of the FreeBSD Subversion repository (at least the documentation part). This can be done by running:

```
% svn checkout https://svn.FreeBSD.org/doc/head/ head
```

svn.FreeBSD.org is a public SVN server. Verify the server certificate from the list of Subversion mirror sites.

> Note
>
> This will require the devel/subversion package to be installed.

You should be comfortable using svn. This will allow you to see what has changed between different versions of the files that make up the documentation.

For example, to view the differences between revisions r33733 and r33734 of en_US.ISO8859-1/books/fdp-primer/book.xml , run:

```
% svn diff -r 33733:33734 en_US.ISO8859-1/books/fdp-primer/book.xml
```

Q: How do I find out who else might be translating to the same language?

A: The Documentation Project translations page lists the translation efforts that are currently known about. If others are already working on translating documentation to your language, please do not duplicate their efforts. Instead, contact them to see how you can help.

If no one is listed on that page as translating for your language, then send a message to the FreeBSD documentation project mailing list in case someone else is thinking of doing a translation, but has not announced it yet.

Q: No one else is translating to my language. What do I do?

A: Congratulations, you have just started the "FreeBSD *your-language-here* Documentation Translation Project". Welcome aboard.

First, decide whether or not you have got the time to spare. Since you are the only person working on your language at the moment it is going to be your responsibility to publicize your work and coordinate any volunteers that might want to help you.

Write an email to the Documentation Project mailing list, announcing that you are going to translate the documentation, so the Documentation Project translations page can be maintained.

If there is already someone in your country providing FreeBSD mirroring services you should contact them and ask if you can have some webspace for your project, and possibly an email address or mailing list services.

Then pick a document and start translating. It is best to start with something fairly small—either the FAQ, or one of the tutorials.

Q: I have translated some documentation, where do I send it?

A: That depends. If you are already working with a translation team (such as the Japanese team, or the German team) then they will have their own procedures for handling submitted documentation, and these will be outlined on their web pages.

If you are the only person working on a particular language (or you are responsible for a translation project and want to submit your changes back to the FreeBSD project) then you should send your translation to the FreeBSD project (see the next question).

Q: I am the only person working on translating to this language, how do I submit my translation?

or

We are a translation team, and want to submit documentation that our members have translated for us.

A: First, make sure your translation is organized properly. This means that it should drop into the existing documentation tree and build straight away.

Currently, the FreeBSD documentation is stored in a top level directory called head/. Directories below this are named according to the language code they are written in, as defined in ISO639 (/usr/share/misc/ iso639 on a version of FreeBSD newer than 20th January 1999).

If your language can be encoded in different ways (for example, Chinese) then there should be directories below this, one for each encoding format you have provided.

Finally, you should have directories for each document.

For example, a hypothetical Swedish translation might look like:

```
head/
    sv_SE.ISO8859-1/
```

```
                    Makefile
                    htdocs/
                            docproj/
                    books/
                            faq/
                                    Makefile
                                    book.xml
```

sv_SE.ISO8859-1 is the name of the translation, in *lang*.*encoding* form. Note the two Makefiles, which will be used to build the documentation.

Use tar(1) and gzip(1) to compress up your documentation, and send it to the project.

```
% cd doc
% tar cf swedish-docs.tar sv_SE.ISO8859-1
% gzip -9 swedish-docs.tar
```

Put swedish-docs.tar.gz somewhere. If you do not have access to your own webspace (perhaps your ISP does not let you have any) then you can email Documentation Engineering Team <doceng@FreeBSD.org>, and arrange to email the files when it is convenient.

Either way, you should use Bugzilla to submit a report indicating that you have submitted the documentation. It would be very helpful if you could get other people to look over your translation and double check it first, since it is unlikely that the person committing it will be fluent in the language.

Someone (probably the Documentation Project Manager, currently Documentation Engineering Team <doceng@FreeBSD.org>) will then take your translation and confirm that it builds. In particular, the following things will be looked at:

1. Do all your files use RCS strings (such as "ID")?

2. Does make all in the sv_SE.ISO8859-1 directory work correctly?

3. Does make install work correctly?

If there are any problems then whoever is looking at the submission will get back to you to work them out.

If there are no problems your translation will be committed as soon as possible.

Q: Can I include language or country specific text in my translation?

A: We would prefer that you did not.

For example, suppose that you are translating the Handbook to Korean, and want to include a section about retailers in Korea in your Handbook.

There is no real reason why that information should not be in the English (or German, or Spanish, or Japanese, or ...) versions as well. It is feasible that an English speaker in Korea might try to pick up a copy of FreeBSD whilst over there. It also helps increase FreeBSD's perceived presence around the globe, which is not a bad thing.

If you have country specific information, please submit it as a change to the English Handbook (using Bugzilla) and then translate the change back to your language in the translated Handbook.

Thanks.

Q: How should language specific characters be included?

A: Non-ASCII characters in the documentation should be included using SGML entities.

Briefly, these look like an ampersand (&), the name of the entity, and a semi-colon (;).

The entity names are defined in ISO8879, which is in the ports tree as textproc/iso8879.

A few examples include:
Entity: é
Appearance: é
Description: Small "e" with an acute accent
Entity: É
Appearance: É
Description: Large "E" with an acute accent
Entity: ü
Appearance: ü
Description: Small "u" with an umlaut

After you have installed the iso8879 port, the files in `/usr/local/share/xml/iso8879` contain the complete list.

Q: Addressing the reader

A: In the English documents, the reader is addressed as "you", there is no formal/informal distinction as there is in some languages.

If you are translating to a language which does distinguish, use whichever form is typically used in other technical documentation in your language. If in doubt, use a mildly polite form.

Q: Do I need to include any additional information in my translations?

A: Yes.

The header of the English version of each document will look something like this:

```
<!--

    The FreeBSD Documentation Project

    $FreeBSD: head/en_US.ISO8859-1/books/faq/book.xml 38674 2012-04-14 13:52:52Z $
-->
```

The exact boilerplate may change, but it will always include a $FreeBSD$ line and the phrase `The FreeBSD Documentation Project`. Note that the $FreeBSD part is expanded automatically by Subversion, so it should be empty (just `$FreeBSD$`) for new files.

Your translated documents should include their own $FreeBSD$ line, and change the `FreeBSD Documentation Project` line to `The FreeBSD language Documentation Project`.

In addition, you should add a third line which indicates which revision of the English text this is based on.

So, the Spanish version of this file might start:

```
<!--

    The FreeBSD Spanish Documentation Project

    $FreeBSD: head/es_ES.ISO8859-1/books/faq/book.xml 38826 2012-05-17 19:12:14Z ↺
hrs $
    Original revision: r38674
-->
```

Chapter 12. PO Translations

12.1. Introduction

The GNU gettext system offers translators an easy way to create and maintain translations of documents. Translatable strings are extracted from the original document into a PO (Portable Object) file. Translated versions of the strings are entered with a separate editor. The strings can be used directly or built into a complete translated version of the original document.

12.2. Quick Start

The procedure shown in Section 1.1, "Quick Start" is assumed to have already been performed, but the TRANSLATOR option must be enabled in the textproc/docproj port. If that option was not enabled, display the options menu and enable it, then reinstall the port:

```
# cd /usr/ports/textproc/docproj
# make config
# make clean deinstall install clean
```

This example shows the creation of a Spanish translation of the short Leap Seconds article.

Procedure 12.1. Install a PO Editor

• A PO editor is needed to edit translation files. This example uses editors/poedit.

```
# cd /usr/ports/editors/poedit
# make install clean
```

Procedure 12.2. Initial Setup

When a new translation is first created, the directory structure and Makefile must be created or copied from the English original:

1. Create a directory for the new translation. The English article source is in ~/doc/en_US.ISO8859-1/articles/leap-seconds/ . The Spanish translation will go in ~/doc/es_ES.ISO8859-1/articles/leap-seconds/. The path is the same except for the name of the language directory.

   ```
   % svn mkdir --parents ~/doc/es_ES.ISO8859-1/articles/leap-seconds/
   ```

2. Copy the Makefile from the original document into the translation directory:

   ```
   % svn cp ~/doc/en_US.ISO8859-1/articles/leap-seconds/Makefile \
       ~/doc/es_ES.ISO8859-1/articles/leap-seconds/
   ```

Procedure 12.3. Translation

Translating a document consists of two steps: extracting translatable strings from the original document, and entering translations for those strings. These steps are repeated until the translator feels that enough of the document has been translated to produce a usable translated document.

1. Extract the translatable strings from the original English version into a PO file:

   ```
   % cd ~/doc/es_ES.ISO8859-1/articles/leap-seconds/
   % make po
   ```

2. Use a PO editor to enter translations in the PO file. There are several different editors available. poedit from editors/poedit is shown here.

The PO file name is the two-character language code followed by an underline and a two-character region code. For Spanish, the file name is es_ES.po .

```
% poedit es_ES.po
```

Procedure 12.4. Generating a Translated Document

1. Generate the translated document:

```
% cd ~/doc/es_ES.ISO8859-1/articles/leap-seconds/
% make tran
```

The name of the generated document matches the name of the English original, usually article.xml for articles or book.xml for books.

2. Check the generated file by rendering it to HTML and viewing it with a web browser:

```
% make FORMATS=html
% firefox article.html
```

12.3. Creating New Translations

The first step to creating a new translated document is locating or creating a directory to hold it. FreeBSD puts translated documents in a subdirectory named for their language and region in the format *lang_REGION*. *lang* is a two-character lowercase code. It is followed by an underscore character and then the two-character uppercase *REGION* code.

Table 12.1. Language Names

Language	Region	Translated Directory Name	PO File Name	Character Set
English	United States	en_US.ISO8859-1	en_US.po	ISO 8859-1
Bengali	Bangladesh	bn_BD.UTF-8	bn_BD.po	UTF-8
Danish	Denmark	da_DK.ISO8859-1	da_DK.po	ISO 8859-1
German	Germany	de_DE.ISO8859-1	de_DE.po	ISO 8859-1
Greek	Greece	el_GR.ISO8859-7	el_GR.po	ISO 8859-7
Spanish	Spain	es_ES.ISO8859-1	es_ES.po	ISO 8859-1
French	France	fr_FR.ISO8859-1	fr_FR.po	ISO 8859-1
Hungarian	Hungary	hu_HU.ISO8859-2	hu_HU.po	ISO 8859-2
Italian	Italy	it_IT.ISO8859-15	it_IT.po	ISO 8859-15
Japanese	Japan	ja_JP.eucJP	ja_JP.po	EUC JP
Korean	Korea	ko_KR.UTF-8	ko_KR.po	UTF-8
Mongolian	Mongolia	mn_MN.UTF-8	mn_MN.po	UTF-8
Dutch	Netherlands	nl_NL.ISO8859-1	nl_NL.po	ISO 8859-1
Norwegian	Norway	no_NO.ISO8859-1	no_NO.po	ISO 8859-1
Polish	Poland	pl_PL.ISO8859-2	pl_PL.po	ISO 8859-2
Portuguese	Brazil	pt_BR.ISO8859-1	pt_BR.po	ISO 8859-1
Russian	Russia	ru_RU.KOI8-R	ru_RU.po	KOI8-R
Serbian	Serbia	sr_YU.ISO8859-2	sr_YU.po	ISO 8859-2

Language	Region	Translated Directory Name	PO File Name	Character Set
Turkish	Turkey	`tr_TR.ISO8859-9`	`tr_TR.po`	ISO 8859-9
Chinese	China	`zh_CN.UTF-8`	`zh_CN.po`	UTF-8
Chinese	Taiwan	`zh_TW.UTF-8`	`zh_TW.po`	UTF-8

The translations are in subdirectories of the main documentation directory, here assumed to be ~/doc/ as shown in Section 1.1, "Quick Start". For example, German translations are located in ~/doc/de_DE.ISO8859-1/ , and French translations are in ~/doc/fr_FR.ISO8859-1/ .

Each language directory contains separate subdirectories named for the type of documents, usually `articles/` and `books/`.

Combining these directory names gives the complete path to an article or book. For example, the French translation of the NanoBSD article is in ~/doc/fr_FR.ISO8859-1/articles/nanobsd/ , and the Mongolian translation of the Handbook is in ~/doc/mn_MN.UTF-8/books/handbook/ .

A new language directory must be created when translating a document to a new language. If the language directory already exists, only a subdirectory in the `articles/` or `books/` directory is needed.

FreeBSD documentation builds are controlled by a `Makefile` in the same directory. With simple articles, the `Makefile` can often just be copied verbatim from the original English directory. The translation process combines multiple separate `book.xml` and `chapter.xml` files in books into a single file, so the `Makefile` for book translations must be copied and modified.

Example 12.1. Creating a Spanish Translation of the Porter's Handbook

Create a new Spanish translation of the Porter's Handbook. The original is a book in ~/doc/en_US.ISO8859-1/books/porters-handbook/ .

1. The Spanish language books directory ~/doc/es_ES.ISO8859-1/books/ already exists, so only a new subdirectory for the Porter's Handbook is needed:

   ```
   % cd ~/doc/es_ES.ISO8859-1/books/
   % svn mkdir porters-handbook
   A         porters-handbook
   ```

2. Copy the `Makefile` from the original book:

   ```
   % cd ~/doc/es_ES.ISO8859-1/books/porters-handbook
   % svn cp ~/doc/en_US.ISO8859-1/books/porters-handbook/Makefile .
   A         Makefile
   ```

   Modify the contents of the `Makefile` to only expect a single `book.xml` :

   ```
   #
   # $FreeBSD$
   #
   # Build the FreeBSD Porter's Handbook.
   #

   MAINTAINER=doc@FreeBSD.org

   DOC?= book

   FORMATS?= html-split

   INSTALL_COMPRESSED?= gz
   INSTALL_ONLY_COMPRESSED?=
   ```

```
# XML content
SRCS=  book.xml

# Images from the cross-document image library
IMAGES_LIB+=      callouts/1.png
IMAGES_LIB+=      callouts/2.png
IMAGES_LIB+=      callouts/3.png
IMAGES_LIB+=      callouts/4.png
IMAGES_LIB+=      callouts/5.png
IMAGES_LIB+=      callouts/6.png
IMAGES_LIB+=      callouts/7.png
IMAGES_LIB+=      callouts/8.png
IMAGES_LIB+=      callouts/9.png
IMAGES_LIB+=      callouts/10.png
IMAGES_LIB+=      callouts/11.png
IMAGES_LIB+=      callouts/12.png
IMAGES_LIB+=      callouts/13.png
IMAGES_LIB+=      callouts/14.png
IMAGES_LIB+=      callouts/15.png
IMAGES_LIB+=      callouts/16.png
IMAGES_LIB+=      callouts/17.png
IMAGES_LIB+=      callouts/18.png
IMAGES_LIB+=      callouts/19.png
IMAGES_LIB+=      callouts/20.png
IMAGES_LIB+=      callouts/21.png

URL_RELPREFIX?= ../../../..
DOC_PREFIX?= ${.CURDIR}/../../..

.include "${DOC_PREFIX}/share/mk/doc.project.mk"
```

Now the document structure is ready for the translator to begin translating with `make po`.

Example 12.2. Creating a French Translation of the PGP Keys Article

Create a new French translation of the PGP Keys article. The original is an article in `~/doc/en_US.ISO8859-1/articles/pgpkeys/`.

1. The French language article directory `~/doc/fr_FR.ISO8859-1/articles/` already exists, so only a new subdirectory for the PGP Keys article is needed:

```
% cd ~/doc/fr_FR.ISO8859-1/articles/
% svn mkdir pgpkeys
A         pgpkeys
```

2. Copy the `Makefile` from the original article:

```
% cd ~/doc/fr_FR.ISO8859-1/articles/pgpkeys
% svn cp ~/doc/en_US.ISO8859-1/articles/pgpkeys/Makefile .
A         Makefile
```

Check the contents of the `Makefile`. Because this is a simple article, in this case the `Makefile` can be used unchanged. The `$FreeBSD...$` version string on the second line will be replaced by the version control system when this file is committed.

```
#
# $FreeBSD$
#
# Article: PGP Keys
```

```
DOC?= article

FORMATS?= html
WITH_ARTICLE_TOC?= YES

INSTALL_COMPRESSED?= gz
INSTALL_ONLY_COMPRESSED?=

SRCS=   article.xml

# To build with just key fingerprints, set FINGERPRINTS_ONLY.

URL_RELPREFIX?= ../../../..
DOC_PREFIX?=    ${.CURDIR}/../../..

.include "${DOC_PREFIX}/share/mk/doc.project.mk"
```

With the document structure complete, the PO file can be created with make po.

12.4. Translating

The gettext system greatly reduces the number of things that must be tracked by a translator. Strings to be translated are extracted from the original document into a PO file. Then a PO editor is used to enter the translated versions of each string.

The FreeBSD PO translation system does not overwrite PO files, so the extraction step can be run at any time to update the PO file.

A PO editor is used to edit the file. editors/poedit is shown in these examples because it is simple and has minimal requirements. Other PO editors offer features to make the job of translating easier. The Ports Collection offers several of these editors, including devel/gtranslator.

It is important to preserve the PO file. It contains all of the work that translators have done.

Example 12.3. Translating the Porter's Handbook to Spanish

Enter Spanish translations of the contents of the Porter's Handbook.

1. Change to the Spanish Porter's Handbook directory and update the PO file. The generated PO file is called es_ES.po as shown in Table 12.1, "Language Names".

    ```
    % cd ~/doc/es_ES.ISO8859-1/books/porters-handbook
    % make po
    ```

2. Enter translations using a PO editor:

    ```
    % poedit es_ES.po
    ```

12.5. Tips for Translators

12.5.1. Preserving XML Tags

Preserve XML tags that are shown in the English original.

Example 12.4. Preserving XML Tags

English original:

```
If <acronym>NTP</acronym> is not being used
```

Spanish translation:

```
Si <acronym>NTP</acronym> no se utiliza
```

12.5.2. Preserving Spaces

Preserve existing spaces at the beginning and end of strings to be translated. The translated version must have these spaces also.

12.5.3. Verbatim Tags

The contents of some tags should be copied verbatim, not translated:

- `<citerefentry>`

- `<command>`

- `<filename>`

- `<literal>`

- `<manvolnum>`

- `<orgname>`

- `<package>`

- `<programlisting>`

- `<prompt>`

- `<refentrytitle>`

- `<screen>`

- `<userinput>`

- `<varname>`

12.5.4. $FreeBSD$ Strings

The $FreeBSD$ version strings used in files require special handling. In examples like Example 12.1, "Creating a Spanish Translation of the Porter's Handbook", these strings are not meant to be expanded. The English documents use $ entities to avoid including actual literal dollar signs in the file:

```
&dollar;FreeBSD&dollar;
```

The $ entities are not seen as dollar signs by the version control system and so the string is not expanded into a version string.

When a PO file is created, the $ entities used in examples are replaced with actual dollar signs. The resulting literal $FreeBSD$ string will be wrongly expanded by the version control system when the file is committed.

The same technique as used in the English documents can be used in the translation. The $ is used to replace the dollar sign in the translation entered into the PO editor:

```
&dollar;FreeBSD&dollar;
```

12.6. Building a Translated Document

A translated version of the original document can be created at any time. Any untranslated portions of the original will be included in English in the resulting document. Most PO editors have an indicator that shows how much of the translation has been completed. This makes it easy for the translator to see when enough strings have been translated to make building the final document worthwhile.

Example 12.5. Building the Spanish Porter's Handbook

Build and preview the Spanish version of the Porter's Handbook that was created in an earlier example.

1. Build the translated document. Because the original is a book, the generated document is book.xml .

   ```
   % cd ~/doc/es_ES.ISO8859-1/books/porters-handbook
   % make tran
   ```

2. Render the translated book.xml to HTML and view it with Firefox. This is the same procedure used with the English version of the documents, and other FORMATS can be used here in the same way. See Table 5.1, "Common Output Formats".

   ```
   % make FORMATS=html
   % firefox book.html
   ```

12.7. Submitting the New Translation

Prepare the new translation files for submission. This includes adding the files to the version control system, setting additional properties on them, then creating a diff for submission.

The diff files created by these examples can be attached to a documentation bug report or code review.

Example 12.6. Spanish Translation of the NanoBSD Article

1. Add a FreeBSD version string comment as the first line of the PO file:

   ```
   #$FreeBSD$
   ```

2. Add the Makefile, the PO file, and the generated XML translation to version control:

   ```
   % cd ~/doc/es_ES.ISO8859-1/articles/nanobsd/
   % ls
   Makefile article.xml es_ES.po
   % svn add Makefile article.xml es_ES.po
   A          Makefile
   A          article.xml
   ```

```
A          es_ES.po
```

3. Set the Subversion svn:keywords properties on these files to FreeBSD=%H so $FreeBSD$ strings are expanded into the path, revision, date, and author when committed:

    ```
    % svn propset svn:keywords FreeBSD=%H Makefile article.xml es_ES.po
    property 'svn:keywords' set on 'Makefile'
    property 'svn:keywords' set on 'article.xml'
    property 'svn:keywords' set on 'es_ES.po'
    ```

4. Set the MIME types of the files. These are text/xml for books and articles, and text/x-get-text-translation for the PO file.

    ```
    % svn propset svn:mime-type text/x-gettext-translation es_ES.po
    property 'svn:mime-type' set on 'es_ES.po'
    % svn propset svn:mime-type text/xml article.xml
    property 'svn:mime-type' set on 'article.xml'
    ```

5. Create a diff of the new files from the ~/doc/ base directory so the full path is shown with the filenames. This helps committers identify the target language directory.

    ```
    % cd ~/doc
    svn diff es_ES.ISO8859-1/articles/nanobsd/ > /tmp/es_nanobsd.diff
    ```

Example 12.7. Korean UTF-8 Translation of the Explaining-BSD Article

1. Add a FreeBSD version string comment as the first line of the PO file:

    ```
    #$FreeBSD$
    ```

2. Add the Makefile, the PO file, and the generated XML translation to version control:

    ```
    % cd ~/doc/ko_KR.UTF-8/articles/explaining-bsd/
    % ls
    Makefile article.xml ko_KR.po
    % svn add Makefile article.xml ko_KR.po
    A          Makefile
    A          article.xml
    A          ko_KR.po
    ```

3. Set the Subversion svn:keywords properties on these files to FreeBSD=%H so $FreeBSD$ strings are expanded into the path, revision, date, and author when committed:

    ```
    % svn propset svn:keywords FreeBSD=%H Makefile article.xml ko_KR.po
    property 'svn:keywords' set on 'Makefile'
    property 'svn:keywords' set on 'article.xml'
    property 'svn:keywords' set on 'ko_KR.po'
    ```

4. Set the MIME types of the files. Because these files use the UTF-8 character set, that is also specified. To prevent the version control system from mistaking these files for binary data, the fbsd:notbinary property is also set:

    ```
    % svn propset svn:mime-type 'text/x-gettext-translation; charset=UTF-8' ko_KR.po
    property 'svn:mime-type' set on 'ko_KR.po'
    % svn propset fbsd:notbinary yes ko_KR.po
    property 'fbsd:notbinary' set on 'ko_KR.po'
    % svn propset svn:mime-type 'text/xml; charset=UTF-8' article.xml
    property 'svn:mime-type' set on 'article.xml'
    % svn propset fbsd:notbinary yes article.xml
    ```

```
property 'fbsd:notbinary' set on 'article.xml'
```

5. Create a diff of these new files from the ~/doc/ base directory:

```
% cd ~/doc
svn diff ko_KR.UTF-8/articles/explaining-bsd > /tmp/ko-explaining.diff
```

Chapter 13. Manual Pages

13.1. Introduction

Manual pages, commonly shortened to *man pages*, were conceived as readily-available reminders for command syntax, device driver details, or configuration file formats. They have become an extremely valuable quick-reference from the command line for users, system administrators, and programmers.

Although intended as reference material rather than tutorials, the EXAMPLES sections of manual pages often provide detailed use case.

Manual pages are generally shown interactively by the man(1) command. When the user types man ls, a search is performed for a manual page matching ls. The first matching result is displayed.

13.2. Sections

Manual pages are grouped into *sections*. Each section contains manual pages for a specific category of documentation:

Section Number	Category
1	General Commands
2	System Calls
3	Library Functions
4	Kernel Interfaces
5	File Formats
6	Games
7	Miscellaneous
8	System Manager
9	Kernel Developer

13.3. Markup

Various markup forms and rendering programs have been used for manual pages. FreeBSD has used groff(7) and the newer mandoc(1). Most existing FreeBSD manual pages, and all new ones, use the mdoc(7) form of markup. This is a simple line-based markup that is reasonably expressive. It is mostly semantic: parts of text are marked up for what they are, rather than for how they should appear when rendered. There is some appearance-based markup which is usually best avoided.

Manual page source is usually interpreted and displayed to the screen interactively. The source files can be ordinary text files or compressed with gzip(1) to save space.

Manual pages can also be rendered to other formats, including PostScript for printing or PDF generation. See man(1).

Tip

Testing a new manual page can be challenging when it is not located in the normal manual page search path. man(1) also does not look in the current directory. If the new manual page is in the current directory, prefix the filename with a ./:

```
% man ./mynewmanpage.8
```

An absolute path can also be used:

```
% man /home/xsmith/mynewmanpage.8
```

13.3.1. Manual Page Sections

Manual pages are composed of several standard sections. Each section has a title in upper case, and the sections for a particular type of manual page appear in a specific order. For a category 1 General Command manual page, the sections are:

Section Name	Description
NAME	Name of the command
SYNOPSIS	Format of options and arguments
DESCRIPTION	Description of purpose and usage
ENVIRONMENT	Environment settings that affect operation
EXIT STATUS	Error codes returned on exit
EXAMPLES	Examples of usage
COMPATIBILITY	Compatibility with other implementations
SEE ALSO	Cross-reference to related manual pages
STANDARDS	Compatibility with standards like POSIX
HISTORY	History of implementation
BUGS	Known bugs
AUTHORS	People who created the command or wrote the manual page.

Some sections are optional, and the combination of sections for a specific type of manual page vary. Examples of the most common types are shown later in this chapter.

13.3.2. Macros

mdoc(7) markup is based on *macros*. Lines that begin with a dot contain macro commands, each two or three letters long. For example, consider this portion of the ls(1) manual page:

```
.Dd December 1, 2015  ❶
.Dt LS 1
.Sh NAME  ❷
.Nm ls
.Nd list directory contents
.Sh SYNOPSIS  ❸
.Nm  ❹
.Op Fl -libxo  ❺
.Op Fl ABCFGHILPRSTUWZabcdfghiklmnopqrstuwxy1,  ❻
```

```
.Op Fl D Ar format  ❼
.Op Ar  ❽
.Sh DESCRIPTION  ❾
For each operand that names a
.Ar file
of a type other than
directory,
.Nm
displays its name as well as any requested,
associated information.
For each operand that names a
.Ar file
of type directory,
.Nm
displays the names of files contained
within that directory, as well as any requested, associated
information.
```

❶ A *Document date* and *Document title* are defined.

❷ A *Section header* for the NAME section is defined. Then the *Name* of the command and a one-line *Name description* are defined.

❸ The SYNOPSIS section begins. This section describes the command-line options and arguments accepted.

❹ *Name* (.Nm) has already been defined, and repeating it here just displays the defined value in the text.

❺ An *Optional Flag* called -libxo is shown. The Fl macro adds a dash to the beginning of flags, so this appears in the manual page as --libxo.

❻ A long list of optional single-character flags are shown.

❼ An optional -D flag is defined. If the -D flag is given, it must be followed by an *Argument*. The argument is a *format*, a string that tells ls(1) what to display and how to display it. Details on the format string are given later in the manual page.

❽ A final optional argument is defined. Because no name is specified for the argument, the default of file ... is used.

❾ The *Section header* for the DESCRIPTION section is defined.

When rendered with the command man ls, the result displayed on the screen looks like this:

```
LS(1)                    FreeBSD General Commands Manual                   LS(1)

NAME
     ls – list directory contents

SYNOPSIS
     ls [--libxo] [-ABCFGHILPRSTUWZabcdfghiklmnopqrstuwxy1,] [-D format]
        [file ...-]

DESCRIPTION
     For each operand that names a file of a type other than directory, ls
     displays its name as well as any requested, associated information.  For
     each operand that names a file of type directory, ls displays the names
     of files contained within that directory, as well as any requested,
     associated information.
```

Optional values are shown inside square brackets.

13.3.3. Markup Guidelines

The mdoc(7) markup language is not very strict. For clarity and consistency, the FreeBSD Documentation project adds some additional style guidelines:

Only the first letter of macros is upper case
>   Always use upper case for the first letter of a macro and lower case for the remaining letters.

Begin new sentences on new lines
>   Start a new sentence on a new line, do not begin it on the same line as an existing sentence.

Update `.Dd` when making non-trivial changes to a manual page
> The *Document date* informs the reader about the last time the manual page was updated. It is important to update whenever non-trivial changes are made to the manual pages. Trivial changes like spelling or punctuation fixes that do not affect usage can be made without updating `.Dd`.

Give examples
> Show the reader examples when possible. Even trivial examples are valuable, because what is trivial to the writer is not necessarily trivial to the reader. Three examples are a good goal. A trivial example shows the minimal requirements, a serious example shows actual use, and an in-depth example demonstrates unusual or non-obvious functionality.

Include the BSD license
> Include the BSD license on new manual pages. The preferred license is available from the Committer's Guide.

13.3.4. Markup Tricks

Add a space before punctuation on a line with macros. Example:

```
.Sh SEE ALSO
.Xr geom 4 ,
.Xr boot0cfg 8 ,
.Xr geom 8 ,
.Xr gptboot 8
```

Note how the commas at the end of the `.Xr` lines have been placed after a space. The `.Xr` macro expects two parameters to follow it, the name of an external manual page, and a section number. The space separates the punctuation from the section number. Without the space, the external links would incorrectly point to section 4, or 8,.

13.3.5. Important Macros

Some very common macros will be shown here. For more usage examples, see mdoc(7), groff_mdoc(7), or search for actual use in `/usr/share/man/man*` directories. For example, to search for examples of the `.Bd` *Begin display* macro:

```
% find /usr/share/man/man* | xargs zgrep '.Bd'
```

13.3.5.1. Organizational Macros

Some macros are used to define logical blocks of a manual page.

Organizational Macro	Use
.Sh	Section header. Followed by the name of the section, traditionally all upper case. Think of these as chapter titles.
.Ss	Subsection header. Followed by the name of the subsection. Used to divide a .Sh section into subsections.
.Bl	Begin list. Start a list of items.
.El	End a list.
.Bd	Begin display. Begin a special area of text, like an indented area.
.Ed	End display.

13.3.5.2. Inline Macros

Many macros are used to mark up inline text.

Inline Macro	Use
.Nm	Name. Called with a name as a parameter on the first use, then used later without the parameter to display the name that has already been defined.
.Pa	Path to a file. Used to mark up filenames and directory paths.

13.4. Sample Manual Page Structures

This section shows minimal desired man page contents for several common categories of manual pages.

13.4.1. Section 1 or 8 Command

The preferred basic structure for a section 1 or 8 command:

```
.Dd August 25, 2017
.Dt EXAMPLECMD 8
.Os
.Sh NAME
.Nm examplecmd
.Nd "command to demonstrate section 1 and 8 man pages"
.Sh SYNOPSIS
.Nm
.Op Fl v
.Sh DESCRIPTION
The
.Nm
utility does nothing except demonstrate a trivial but complete
manual page for a section 1 or 8 command.
.Sh SEE ALSO
.Xr exampleconf 5
.Sh AUTHORS
.An Firstname Lastname Aq Mt flastname@example.com
```

13.4.2. Section 4 Device Driver

The preferred basic structure for a section 4 device driver:

```
.Dd August 25, 2017
.Dt EXAMPLEDRIVER 4
.Os
.Sh NAME
.Nm exampledriver
.Nd "driver to demonstrate section 4 man pages"
.Sh SYNOPSIS
To compile this driver into the kernel, add this line to the
kernel configuration file:
.Bd -ragged -offset indent
.Cd "device exampledriver"
.Ed
.Pp
To load the driver as a module at boot, add this line to
.Xr loader.conf 5 :
.Bd -literal -offset indent
exampledriver_load="YES"
.Ed
.Sh DESCRIPTION
The
.Nm
driver provides an opportunity to show a skeleton or template
file for section 4 manual pages.
```

```
.Sh HARDWARE
The
.Nm
driver supports these cards from the aptly-named Nonexistent
Technologies:
.Pp
.Bl -bullet -compact
.It
NT X149.2 (single and dual port)
.It
NT X149.8 (single port)
.El
.Sh DIAGNOSTICS
.Bl -diag
.It "flashing green light"
Something bad happened.
.It "flashing red light"
Something really bad happened.
.It "solid black light"
Power cord is unplugged.
.El
.Sh SEE ALSO
.Xr example 8
.Sh HISTORY
The
.Nm
device driver first appeared in
.Fx 49.2 .
.Sh AUTHORS
.An Firstname Lastname Aq Mt flastname@example.com
```

13.4.3. Section 5 Configuration File

The preferred basic structure for a section 5 configuration file:

```
.Dd August 25, 2017
.Dt EXAMPLECONF 5
.Os
.Sh NAME
.Nm example.conf
.Nd "config file to demonstrate section 5 man pages"
.Sh DESCRIPTION
.Nm
is an example configuration file.
.Sh SEE ALSO
.Xr example 8
.Sh AUTHORS
.An Firstname Lastname Aq Mt flastname@example.com
```

13.5. Example Manual Pages to Use as Templates

Some manual pages are suitable as in-depth examples.

Manual Page	Path to Source Location
cp(1)	/usr/src/bin/cp/cp.1
vt(4)	/usr/src/share/man/man4/vt.4
crontab(5)	/usr/src/usr.sbin/cron/crontab/crontab.5
gpart(8)	/usr/src/sbin/geom/class/part/gpart.8

13.6. Resources

Resources for manual page writers:

- man(1)

- mandoc(1)

- groff_mdoc(7)

- Practical UNIX Manuals: mdoc

- History of UNIX Manpages

Chapter 14. Writing Style

14.1. Tips

Technical documentation can be improved by consistent use of several principles. Most of these can be classified into three goals: *be clear*, *be complete*, and *be concise*. These goals can conflict with each other. Good writing consists of a balance between them.

14.1.1. Be Clear

Clarity is extremely important. The reader may be a novice, or reading the document in a second language. Strive for simple, uncomplicated text that clearly explains the concepts.

Avoid flowery or embellished speech, jokes, or colloquial expressions. Write as simply and clearly as possible. Simple text is easier to understand and translate.

Keep explanations as short, simple, and clear as possible. Avoid empty phrases like "in order to", which usually just means "to". Avoid potentially patronizing words like "basically". Avoid Latin terms like "i.e." or "cf.", which may be unknown outside of academic or scientific groups.

Write in a formal style. Avoid addressing the reader as "you". For example, say "copy the file to /tmp" rather than "you can copy the file to /tmp".

Give clear, correct, *tested* examples. A trivial example is better than no example. A good example is better yet. Do not give bad examples, identifiable by apologies or sentences like "but really it should never be done that way". Bad examples are worse than no examples. Give good examples, because *even when warned not to use the example as shown*, the reader will usually just use the example as shown.

Avoid *weasel words* like "should", "might", "try", or "could". These words imply that the speaker is unsure of the facts, and create doubt in the reader.

Similarly, give instructions as imperative commands: not "you should do this", but merely "do this".

14.1.2. Be Complete

Do not make assumptions about the reader's abilities or skill level. Tell them what they need to know. Give links to other documents to provide background information without having to recreate it. Put yourself in the reader's place, anticipate the questions they will ask, and answer them.

14.1.3. Be Concise

While features should be documented completely, sometimes there is so much information that the reader cannot easily find the specific detail needed. The balance between being complete and being concise is a challenge. One approach is to have an introduction, then a "quick start" section that describes the most common situation, followed by an in-depth reference section.

14.2. Guidelines

To promote consistency between the myriad authors of the FreeBSD documentation, some guidelines have been drawn up for authors to follow.

Use American English Spelling
> There are several variants of English, with different spellings for the same word. Where spellings differ, use the American English variant. "color", not "colour", "rationalize", not "rationalise", and so on.

Note

The use of British English may be accepted in the case of a contributed article, however the spelling must be consistent within the whole document. The other documents such as books, web site, manual pages, etc. will have to use American English.

Do not use contractions
 Do not use contractions. Always spell the phrase out in full. "Don't use contractions" is wrong.

 Avoiding contractions makes for a more formal tone, is more precise, and is slightly easier for translators.

Use the serial comma
 In a list of items within a paragraph, separate each item from the others with a comma. Separate the last item from the others with a comma and the word "and".

 For example:

> This is a list of one, two and three items.

 Is this a list of three items, "one", "two", and "three", or a list of two items, "one" and "two and three"?

 It is better to be explicit and include a serial comma:

> This is a list of one, two, and three items.

Avoid redundant phrases
 Do not use redundant phrases. In particular, "the command", "the file", and "man command" are often redundant.

 For example, commands:

 Wrong: Use the `svn` command to update sources.

 Right: Use `svn` to update sources.

 Filenames:

 Wrong: ... in the filename `/etc/rc.local` ...

 Right: ... in `/etc/rc.local` ...

 Manual page references (the second example uses `citerefentry` with the `&man.csh.1;` entity):.

 Wrong: See `man csh` for more information.

 Right: See csh(1).

Two spaces between sentences
 Always use two spaces between sentences, as it improves readability and eases use of tools such as Emacs.

 A period and spaces followed by a capital letter does not always mark a new sentence, especially in names. "Jordan K. Hubbard" is a good example. It has a capital H following a period and a space, and is certainly not a new sentence.

For more information about writing style, see Elements of Style, by William Strunk.

14.3. Style Guide

To keep the source for the documentation consistent when many different people are editing it, please follow these style conventions.

14.3.1. Letter Case

Tags are entered in lower case, `para`, *not* `PARA`.

Text that appears in SGML contexts is generally written in upper case, `<!ENTITY…>`, and `<!DOCTYPE…>`, *not* `<!entity…>` and `<!doctype…>`.

14.3.2. Acronyms

Acronyms should be defined the first time they appear in a document, as in: "Network Time Protocol (NTP)". After the acronym has been defined, use the acronym alone unless it makes more sense contextually to use the whole term. Acronyms are usually defined only once per chapter or per document.

All acronyms should be enclosed in `acronym` tags.

14.3.3. Indentation

The first line in each file starts with no indentation, *regardless* of the indentation level of the file which might contain the current file.

Opening tags increase the indentation level by two spaces. Closing tags decrease the indentation level by two spaces. Blocks of eight spaces at the start of a line should be replaced with a tab. Do not use spaces in front of tabs, and do not add extraneous whitespace at the end of a line. Content within elements should be indented by two spaces if the content runs over more than one line.

For example, the source for this section looks like this:

```
<chapter>
  <title> ...</title>

  <sect1>
    <title> ...</title>

    <sect2>
      <title> Indentation</title>

      <para>The first line in each file starts with no indentation,
  <emphasis> regardless</emphasis> of the indentation level of
  the file which might contain the current file.</para>

      ...
    </sect2>
  </sect1>
</chapter>
```

Tags containing long attributes follow the same rules. Following the indentation rules in this case helps editors and writers see which content is inside the tags:

```
<para>See the <link
    linkend="gmirror-troubleshooting"> Troubleshooting</link>
  section if there are problems booting.  Powering down and
  disconnecting the original <filename> ada0</filename>  disk
  will allow it to be kept as an offline backup.</para>

<para>It is also possible to journal the boot disk of a &os;
  system.  Refer to the article <link
    xlink:href="&url.articles.gjournal-desktop;">  Implementing UFS
```

```
    Journaling on a Desktop PC</link> for detailed
  instructions.</para>
```

When an element is too long to fit on the remainder of a line without wrapping, moving the start tag to the next line can make the source easier to read. In this example, the `systemitem` element has been moved to the next line to avoid wrapping and indenting:

```
<para>With file flags, even
  <systemitem class="username"> root</systemitem>  can be
  prevented from removing or altering files.</para>
```

Configurations to help various text editors conform to these guidelines can be found in Chapter 15, *Editor Configuration*.

14.3.4. Tag Style

14.3.4.1. Tag Spacing

Tags that start at the same indent as a previous tag should be separated by a blank line, and those that are not at the same indent as a previous tag should not:

```
<article lang='en'>
  <articleinfo>
    <title>NIS</title>

    <pubdate> October 1999</pubdate>

    <abstract>
      <para>...
...
...</para>
    </abstract>
  </articleinfo>

  <sect1>
    <title>...</title>

    <para>...</para>
  </sect1>

  <sect1>
    <title>...</title>

    <para>...</para>
  </sect1>
</article>
```

14.3.4.2. Separating Tags

Tags like `itemizedlist` which will always have further tags inside them, and in fact do not take character data themselves, are always on a line by themselves.

Tags like `para` and `term` do not need other tags to contain normal character data, and their contents begin immediately after the tag, *on the same line*.

The same applies to when these two types of tags close.

This leads to an obvious problem when mixing these tags.

When a starting tag which cannot contain character data directly follows a tag of the type that requires other tags within it to use character data, they are on separate lines. The second tag should be properly indented.

When a tag which can contain character data closes directly after a tag which cannot contain character data closes, they co-exist on the same line.

14.3.5. Whitespace Changes

Do not commit changes to content at the same time as changes to formatting.

When content and whitespace changes are kept separate, translation teams can easily see whether a change was content that must be translated or only whitespace.

For example, if two sentences have been added to a paragraph so that the line lengths now go over 80 columns, first commit the change with the too-long lines. Then fix the line wrapping, and commit this second change. In the commit message for the second change, indicate that this is a whitespace-only change that can be ignored by translators.

14.3.6. Non-Breaking Space

Avoid line breaks in places where they look ugly or make it difficult to follow a sentence. Line breaks depend on the width of the chosen output medium. In particular, viewing the HTML documentation with a text browser can lead to badly formatted paragraphs like the next one:

```
Data capacity ranges from 40 MB to 15
GB.  Hardware compression …
```

The general entity   prohibits line breaks between parts belonging together. Use non-breaking spaces in the following places:

- between numbers and units:

  ```
  57600 bps
  ```

- between program names and version numbers:

  ```
  &os; 9.2
  ```

- between multiword names (use with caution when applying this to more than 3-4 word names like "The FreeBSD Brazilian Portuguese Documentation Project"):

  ```
  Sun Microsystems
  ```

14.4. Word List

This list of words shows the correct spelling and capitalization when used in FreeBSD documentation. If a word is not on this list, ask about it on the FreeBSD documentation project mailing list.

Word	XML Code	Notes
CD-ROM	`<acronym> CD-ROM</acronym>`	
DoS (Denial of Service)	`<acronym> DoS</acronym>`	
email		
file system		
IPsec		
Internet		
manual page		
mail server		
name server		
Ports Collection		
read-only		

Word	XML Code	Notes
Soft Updates		
stdin	`<varname>stdin</varname>`	
stdout	`<varname>stdout</varname>`	
stderr	`<varname>stderr</varname>`	
Subversion	`<application>Subversion</application>`	Do not refer to the Subversion application as SVN in upper case. To refer to the command, use `<command>svn</command>`.
UNIX®	`&unix;`	
userland		things that apply to user space, not the kernel
web server		

Chapter 15. Editor Configuration

Adjusting text editor configuration can make working on document files quicker and easier, and help documents conform to FDP guidelines.

15.1. Vim

Install from editors/vim or editors/vim-lite, then follow the configuration instructions in Section 15.1.2, "Configuration".

15.1.1. Use

Press P to reformat paragraphs or text that has been selected in Visual mode. Press T to replace groups of eight spaces with a tab.

15.1.2. Configuration

Edit ~/.vimrc, adding these lines to the end of the file:

```
if has("autocmd")
    au BufNewFile,BufRead *.sgml,*.ent,*.xsl,*.xml call Set_SGML()
    au BufNewFile,BufRead *.[1-9] call ShowSpecial()
endif " has(autocmd)

function Set_Highlights()
    "match ExtraWhitespace /^\s* \s*\|\s\+$/
    highlight default link OverLength ErrorMsg
    match OverLength /\%71v.\+/
    return 0
endfunction

function ShowSpecial()
    setlocal list listchars=tab:>>,trail:*,eol:$
    hi def link nontext ErrorMsg
    return 0
endfunction " ShowSpecial()

function Set_SGML()
    setlocal number
    syn match sgmlSpecial "&[^;]*;"
    setlocal syntax=sgml
    setlocal filetype=xml
    setlocal shiftwidth=2
    setlocal textwidth=70
    setlocal tabstop=8
    setlocal softtabstop=2
    setlocal formatprg="fmt -p"
    setlocal autoindent
    setlocal smartindent
    " Rewrap paragraphs
    noremap P gqj
    " Replace spaces with tabs
    noremap T :s/        /\t/<CR>
    call ShowSpecial()
    call Set_Highlights()
    return 0
endfunction " Set_SGML()
```

15.2. Emacs

Install from editors/emacs or editors/emacs-devel.

15.2.1. Validation

Emacs's nxml-mode uses compact relax NG schemas for validating XML. A compact relax NG schema for FreeBSD's extension to DocBook 5.0 is included in the documentation repository. To configure nxml-mode to validate using this schema, create ~/.emacs.d/schema/schemas.xml and add these lines to the file:

```
<locatingRules xmlns="http://thaiopensource.com/ns/locating-rules/1.0">
  <documentElement localName="section" typeId="DocBook">
  <documentElement localName="chapter" typeId="DocBook">
  <documentElement localName="article" typeId="DocBook">
  <documentElement localName="book" typeId="DocBook">
  <typeId id="DocBook" uri="/usr/local/share/xml/docbook/5.0/rng/docbook.rnc">
</locatingRules>
```

15.2.2. Automated Proofreading with Flycheck and Igor

The Flycheck package is available from Milkypostman's Emacs Lisp Package Archive (MELPA). If MELPA is not already in Emacs's packages-archives, it can be added by evaluating

```
(add-to-list 'package-archives '("melpa" . "http://stable.melpa.org/packages/") t)
```

Add the line to Emacs's initialization file (one of ~/.emacs, ~/.emacs.el, or ~.emacs.d/init.el) to make this change permanent.

To install Flycheck, evaluate

```
(package-install 'flycheck)
```

Create a Flycheck checker for textproc/igor by evaluating

```
(flycheck-define-checker igor
  "FreeBSD Documentation Project sanity checker.

See URLs https://www.freebsd.org/docproj/ and
http://www.freshports.org/textproc/igor/."
  :command ("igor" "-X" source-inplace)
  :error-parser flycheck-parse-checkstyle
  :modes (nxml-mode)
  :standard-input t)

  (add-to-list 'flycheck-checkers 'igor 'append)
```

Again, add these lines to Emacs's initialization file to make the changes permanent.

15.2.3. FreeBSD Documentation Specific Settings

To apply settings specific to the FreeBSD documentation project, create .dir-locals.el in the root directory of the documentation repository and add these lines to the file:

```
;;; Directory Local Variables
;;; For more information see (info "(emacs) Directory Variables")

((nxml-mode
  (eval . (turn-on-auto-fill))
  (fill-column . 70)
  (eval . (require 'flycheck))
  (eval . (flycheck-mode 1))
  (flycheck-checker . igor)
  (eval . (add-to-list 'rng-schema-locating-files "~/.emacs.d/schema/schemas.xml")))))
```

15.3. nano

Install from editors/nano or editors/nano-devel.

15.3.1. Configuration

Copy the sample XML syntax highlight file to the user's home directory:

```
% cp /usr/local/share/nano/xml.nanorc ~/.nanorc
```

Use an editor to replace the lines in the ~/.nanorc syntax "xml" block with these rules:

```
syntax "xml" "\.([jrs]html?|xml|xslt?)$"
# trailing whitespace
color ,blue "[[:space:]]+$"
# multiples of eight spaces at the start a line
# (after zero or more tabs) should be a tab
color ,blue "^([TAB]*[ -]{8})+"
# tabs after spaces
color ,yellow "( )+TAB"
# highlight indents that have an odd number of spaces
color ,red "^(([ -]{2})+|(TAB+))*[ -]{1}[^ -]{1}"
# lines longer than 70 characters
color ,yellow "^(.{71})|(TAB.{63})|(TAB{2}.{55})|(TAB{3}.{47}).+$"
```

Process the file to create embedded tabs:

```
% perl -i'' -pe 's/TAB/\t/g' ~/.nanorc
```

15.3.2. Use

Specify additional helpful options when running the editor:

```
% nano -AKipwz -r 70 -T8 chapter.xml
```

Users of csh(1) can define an alias in ~/.cshrc to automate these options:

```
alias nano "nano -AKipwz -r 70 -T8"
```

After the alias is defined, the options will be added automatically:

```
% nano chapter.xml
```

Chapter 16. See Also

This document is deliberately not an exhaustive discussion of XML, the DTDs listed, and the FreeBSD Documentation Project. For more information about these, you are encouraged to see the following web sites.

16.1. The FreeBSD Documentation Project

- The FreeBSD Documentation Project web pages

- The FreeBSD Handbook

16.2. XML

- W3C's XML page SGML/XML web page

16.3. HTML

- The World Wide Web Consortium

- The HTML 4.0 specification

16.4. DocBook

- The DocBook Technical Committee, maintainers of the DocBook DTD

- DocBook: The Definitive Guide, the online documentation for the DocBook DTD

- The DocBook Open Repository contains DSSSL stylesheets and other resources for people using DocBook

Appendix A. Examples

These examples are not exhaustive—they do not contain all the elements that might be desirable to use, particularly in a document's front matter. For more examples of DocBook markup, examine the XML source for this and other documents available in the Subversion doc repository, or available online starting at `http://svnweb.Free-BSD.org/doc/`.

A.1. DocBook book

Example A.1. DocBook book

```xml
<!DOCTYPE book PUBLIC "-//FreeBSD//DTD DocBook XML V5.0-Based Extension//EN"
 "http://www.FreeBSD.org/XML/share/xml/freebsd50.dtd">

<book xmlns="http://docbook.org/ns/docbook"
  xmlns:xlink="http://www.w3.org/1999/xlink" version="5.0"
  xml:lang="en">

  <info>
    <title>An Example Book</title>

    <author>
      <personname>
        <firstname> Your first name</firstname>
        <surname> Your surname</surname>
      </personname>

      <affiliation>
<address>
  <email> foo@example.com</email>
</address>
      </affiliation>
    </author>

    <copyright>
      <year>2000</year>
      <holder> Copyright string here</holder>
    </copyright>

    <abstract>
      <para>If your book has an abstract then it should go here.</para>
    </abstract>
  </info>

  <preface>
    <title> Preface</title>

    <para>Your book may have a preface, in which case it should be placed
      here.</para>
  </preface>

  <chapter>
    <title>My First Chapter</title>

    <para>This is the first chapter in my book.</para>

    <sect1>
      <title>My First Section</title>

      <para>This is the first section in my book.</para>
```

```
      </sect1>
    </chapter>
  </book>
```

A.2. DocBook `article`

Example A.2. DocBook `article`

```
<!DOCTYPE article PUBLIC "-//FreeBSD//DTD DocBook XML V5.0-Based Extension//EN"
  "http://www.FreeBSD.org/XML/share/xml/freebsd50.dtd">

<article xmlns="http://docbook.org/ns/docbook"
  xmlns:xlink="http://www.w3.org/1999/xlink" version="5.0"
  xml:lang="en">

  <info>
    <title>An Example Article</title>

    <author>
      <personname>
        <firstname> Your first name</firstname>
        <surname> Your surname</surname>
      </personname>

      <affiliation>
  <address>
    <email> foo@example.com</email>
  </address>
      </affiliation>
    </author>

    <copyright>
      <year>2000</year>
      <holder> Copyright string here</holder>
    </copyright>

    <abstract>
      <para>If your article has an abstract then it should go here.</para>
    </abstract>
  </info>

  <sect1>
    <title>My First Section</title>

    <para>This is the first section in my article.</para>

    <sect2>
      <title>My First Sub-Section</title>

      <para>This is the first sub-section in my article.</para>
    </sect2>
  </sect1>
</article>
```

Index

www.ingramcontent.com/pod-product-compliance
Lightning Source LLC
Chambersburg PA
CBHW060153060326
40690CB00018B/4096